The Mirth and Misery of Marriage

The Mirth and Misery of Marriage

LIB UZZELL GRIFFIN

BROADMAN PRESS
Nashville, Tennessee

Scripture quotations marked TLB are from *The Living Bible.* Copyright © Tyndale House Publishers, Wheaton, Illinois, 1971. Used by permission. Scripture quotations marked KJV are from the King James Version of the Bible.

Library of Congress Cataloging-in-Publication Data

Griffin, Lib Uzzell, 1917–
 The mirth and misery of marriage.

  1. Marriage—Anecdotes, facetiae, satire, etc.
I. Title.
HQ734.G795 1988   306.8′1′0207   87-38219
ISBN 0-8054-5733-X

To my many role models—my parents, children, friends, relatives, and strangers who, by example, reaffirm my belief that you *can* be happy, though married. Most of all,
to Chief—
Who makes our marriage what it still is—an adventure!

Contents

Introduction:
The Mirth and Misery of Marriage

I like surprises. I have had plenty in nearly fifty years of marriage to the same man. In fact, he helped write two chapters of this book (#'s 3 and 11). That's what I call a "sir-prize."

I am a creative woman. My major in college was art. After marriage to my best friend, I became very creative. I am the mother of nine children.

I believe life is a heavenly gift. I love the one the Lord gave me. Born prematurely, I almost didn't receive it. It took three ministers to marry me. The knot is tightly tied.

I believe God has a plan for us. With nine children and sixteen grands to date, ours must be to populate the world. It is said, "A baby is God's way of saying He wants the world to go on."

I believe life is to be celebrated. I have tried to celebrate life to the fullest. That, in itself, can age you.

I really dig that Abundant Life. In the mirth and misery of marriage, God has blessed mine with an abundance of mirth.

"Ask and you shall receive" (see Matt. 7:7). I have been asking and receiving, asking and receiving. Dealing with the mirth and misery of marriage, I need all the help I can get. That's what this book is all about. My cup runneth over!

Lib Uzzell Griffin
Durham, North Carolina

1

After Many Blessings and Bothers, Can Chief and Libbylove Find Happiness?

Marriages may be made in heaven, but the survival takes place on earth. I know. I'm a survivor. Not only of nearly five decades of holy wedlock, but of mothering. Mark Twain called children "blessings and bothers." The Good Lord blessed me with nine, seven boys and two girls. Now that calls for mothering.

I had some help. The Lord, in all His wisdom, provided me with a good husband. I call him "Chief." He's Chief of our clan, and made me what I am—a mother.

Shakespeare referred to a matrimonial union as "a world-without-end bargain." Now that will get you to thinking. The word *bargain* has been bandied around so much, you have days when you wonder, *Did I get more than I bargained for in this marriage? Did I get a bargain in my mate? Should I have haggled more? Negotiated? A bargain? A world-without-end bargain? Are you serious? Marriage a contract? Covenant?*

Many people today don't take marriage seriously. There's a department store in our town that carries its wedding gowns in the sporting-goods department.

Marriage is merely a piece of paper to some. Opinions about marriage are a dime a dozen. The participants don't seem to put any more value on their marriage than that. Some couples take shrugging lessons, apathy lessons. "If it doesn't work out, I'll just bail out." Much to certain lawyers' delight.

These easy-come, easy-go marriages don't bother some people. They're like a revolving door. Round and round and finally out they go.

Back on the street, they start looking again. Potential marriage partners are like subways or buses. There's always another one coming along.

It's so bad in our town, we don't send wedding gifts until the couple has been married three years. One bridal shop admits they expect their brides to marry more than once. That's why the store carries only wash-and-wear wedding gowns.

After nearly five decades of marriage to the same guy (my best friend, my playmate) I think it's safe to say: this love relationship is more than a passing fancy.

Somebody asked one movie star, why he waited so late in life to marry. He said that no one had told him how much fun it was. I felt the same way. I never heard about the mirth. Only the misery of marriage.

This attitude is contagious. If you expect your marriage to fail, it will. Add that attitude to the Negative Nellies surrounding us and it's a wonder any marriage makes it. You know the types. Waiting in the wings to spring forth, clucking, "I knew it wouldn't last. Remember I'm the one who told you long ago—'Get rid of the bum. His family has more hang-ups than the telephone company!' " To Negative Nellies, every year is a good "whine" year.

All this badmouthing might be true—if you're a pagan.

Look up. There are your balcony people, your cheerleaders yelling encouragement, "You can make it. Hang in there. The best is yet to come."

Look up higher at your guardian angels. They're chorusing, "Remember your promises. Your covenant. You come from a long line of people who keep their promises. Honor *their* commitments."

Look up even higher, way above your family, friends, and guardian angels. A Fatherly voice urges, "Remember what God has joined together, let no one put asunder."

After nearly five decades, no one can accuse me of thinking matrimony is a joke. I certainly considered the solemnization of marriage a serious event. Solemn is right. My wedding was so solemn the *groom* cried all the way through the ceremony. Not me. I have this irritating, abominable trait of enjoying the moment. Especially a spine-tingling moment. I try to be aware of everything—the time, the place. I soak up every detail. It's no time for tears.

That doesn't mean I'm not appropriately reverent. I take time later to haul out my memories. Then I savour the solemnity, the sacredness of the moment. Privately, at will, I can vividly recall precious moments—exciting, very meaningful. This has helped bring me from the pits to the peaks of my marriage. To concentrate on the mirth, not the misery.

On my wedding day, I knew I was the bride, even if I didn't feel like a bride. I was the only one in white satin. Good thing. Since I am just five feet tall, you might have missed me. Coming down that long aisle was a new experience. I felt more comfortable when my tall, royal-blue-velvet-clad bridesmaids surrounded me.

I had been a reluctant schoolteacher, average artist, embryonic actress, tra la la. But never a bride. It didn't take me long to realize the marital knot was tightly tied. It took three ministers to marry me: a great uncle (the senior man of the cloth should be duly honored), and two uncles who were ministers. Only one was active in the ministry. The other one, confined to a wheelchair, declined. The third minister followed a courtesy custom. We were being married in his church.

One of the wedding ceremony prayers asking for "the gift and heritage of children" certainly was answered. The other prayer I treasure—"that their home may be a blessing and of peace."

These prayers have been answered with bountiful, bouncing babies and a home blessed with more peace than war, more mirth than misery.

Look around you. You'll see marriage is still alive, not just mine but many others. It's not a stale, boring, static, standstill situation. It doesn't have to be uninteresting, boring. Remember—dull, boring, uninteresting things happen to dull, boring, uninteresting people!

In spite of the highly publicized divorce rate, couples continue to marry in increasing numbers. Love and romance are far from dead. They are alive and well. H. L. Mencken (1880-1956), American editor and satirist, said,

> The allurement that women hold out to men is precisely the allurement that Cape Hatteras holds out to sailors. They are enormously dangerous

and hence enormously fascinating. To the average man, doomed to some banal drudgery all his life long, they offer the only grand hazard that he ever encounters. Take them away and his existence would be as flat and secure as that of a moo-cow.

I agree. That's why I say, "Chief makes the living. And I try to make the living worthwhile."

Marriage has been analyzed and criticized but never ignored. Magazines, newspapers, and talk shows abound with advice. *Talk is cheap because supply is great and demand is small.*

Chief declares that our children take everything he's got, *but his advice.* I told him at the time it wasn't wasted. Twenty years later they're telling their own children the same thing.

There is a whole new field of therapists, psychologists, and psychiatrists who're making a good living advising folks about their marriage. Trouble is, they're so young. G. S. Merriman said, "I never take the advice of youngsters because I've been young—but they've never been old."

Advice, they say, is only the approval we seek for something we've decided to do anyway. So why another book on marriage? Marriage has received such bad press. As a newspaper columnist, I hate to admit marriage needs a good PR person. More affirmers. More cheerleaders. More advocates. More motivators. More help.

Why me?

I have asked myself that same question many times. What do I know about marriage? I am a veteran. A survivor. I assure you, you can be happy though married. Like rare cheese, it gets better with age. Hang in there.

Writing's not all that much fun. It's an addiction. The fun is hoping you made someone laugh or gave them a pearl that would help 'em someday.

No, I don't write because it's all fun. It's lonesome. I have to get away by myself. I'm a people person. I'd rather be with Chief, spoiling my sixteen grands, enjoying my own nine children's good company, tending to my own marriage instead of writing about it.

The wedding vows should say, "What God has joined together, let no man, woman, child, sport, or book put asunder."

Am I into self-punishment?

No, a writer has to write. To play the piano or become adept at the sport or hobby of your choice, you must practice. A writer has to feel so deeply, so passionately about something, she has to write about it. Share it.

I feel so deeply, so passionately that marriage is one of God's greatest blessings, as well as bothers, I can't keep it bottled inside. I didn't say it's easy. I said it's an adventure I wouldn't miss for the world.

This book opens on a maturing marriage. Chief and I had been married sixteen years. He was forty-one. I was at the age most people never admit to being over—thirty-nine.

By the book's conclusion, we've logged forty-seven years. So you see, life's never still. Yesterday quickly becomes today now. How did we act or react to this dynamic flow? There's no motion without emotion. So fasten your seat belts, there'll be rough weather once in a while.

Our emotions energize us, so they're not always harmful, something to fear in ourselves, in others. If you don't feel, you might as well be dead. Life's for living. Don't just look *at* life. Look *into* it.

With nine children, I had plenty to celebrate. Surrounded by my blessings, I was happy. I loved being a mom, a homemaker, a "kept" woman, a leisure liver. Glad I married well, I felt like the happy surfer, enjoying the crest of the wave while I could. Knowing nothing lasts forever, I enjoyed my children while I could. The Good Book, remember, never says, ". . . and it came to stay." It says, ". . . and it came to pass." It did. The children were getting ready to fly the coop.

Chief was riding the crest of our matrimonial wave, too. When the book opens, he's enjoying the accomplishments of an earlier period. He is moving out of the Upward and Onward stage to the Consolidation stage. Happy his dental practice is flourishing. He's able, thanks be to God, to support a wife and nine children.

Things have fallen into place for Chief. He's sure of his dental skills and his potential, confident of his ability to manage and to keep a healthy balance between his profession and homework. He has matured and has learned to function smoothly, adequately as a husband and father. You can tell. There's no problem separating an experienced father from the novices. He's the one who, if his child threatens to run away, makes the kid put it in writing!

You can't believe how much smarter Chief becomes with the years. He used to bear his misfortunes like a man—he blamed everything on me, his wife. Now he's faced reality. Marriage is a fifty-fifty proposition. It's amazing how many marriages are on this fifty-fifty basis: he blames her; she blames him. Neither one dares to cast the first stone.

Chief is growing, developing, becoming more well-rounded, flexible, and understanding. In fact, I might have to keep him. He's still plenty of fun. He's learning it's okay to admit you're wrong. He's joined the human race. Relaxed, he can laugh at his foibles. It's a known fact that if you're willing to admit you are all wrong, when you *are* all wrong, you are all right. Chief is all right.

Chief's more patient with me. Kinder. He doesn't fuss and fume when I'm not ready to go out at the appointed time. He keeps a good book nearby. Little volumes like *War and Peace* and *Ivanhoe*. He reads it while he waits. I assure you he's astonished himself at how much he's learned.

2

Libbylove's Balancing Act: Thirty-four Years Juggling Wife and Mother Roles

Stress is often associated with raising your voice, your pulse, and your children.

My stress was self-imposed. This is often the case with most of us. I wanted nine children. I asked for nine children and was blessed with nine children, thanks be to God.

So forget analyzing, criticizing, advertising my motives. It's a well-known fact that I'm an Episcopalian who married a Methodist who went to a Baptist school. I don't advocate a large family for everyone. I happen to believe that God provided me with a great capacity to love. To give of myself. If I had the onesy-twosy family, I would have smothered them to death and made them emotional cripples. My hotel upbringing prepared me for big family life.

If I had birthed nine children all at once it not only would have been a miracle, it would have spurred more research on birth control. Most importantly to me, I could never have managed. One baby at the time allowed me much needed personal growth and time to develop my mothering skills.

Newborns are my special delight. They are heaven's lieutenants. I can spend hours completely mesmerized, never tiring of holding, staring at them, memorizing every feature. They're little wonders, fresh from heaven. They fill me with awe and reverence. I enjoy crooning, "When did you leave Heaven? How could they let you go?" Softly, not only for their sake, but for anyone around. Of all of God's gifts to me, a singing voice was not one of them.

Fascinating as they are, babies don't come with directions. My first book, *The Pains and Pleasures of Parenthood,* chronicles my mothering methods. Especially what I dubbed The Balancing Act: trying to be wife, mother, sister, friend; trying to learn, as a mother, when to let my children go, when to rein 'em in. I call this my Juggling Jester stage.

Having made the decision that motherhood was my desire, I wanted to be the very best mother I could. The Good Book has plenty to say on the subject. After the Bible, would you believe that government pamphlets were the most help?

My library card certainly is a profile of my interests. It never ceases to amaze me how few people remember we have libraries in America. They are chock full of help: encyclopedias, reference volumes, dictionaries, geographies, textbooks, charts, as well as articles and government pamphlets on any subject you need to know more about, including mothering.

If I know the facts and statistics on the subject, have checked the biblical foundation, plus added a dose of my own good common sense, I can save myself a peck of trouble. Most of the time, the mistaken handling of troubles comes from not knowing the facts. I repeat: babies do not come with directions. Nor do husbands.

Now that I have assembled all the needed information, what now? Stop and think. You'll get tired of hearing it, but stop and think I've had to do *ad nauseum.* I'd try to figure out if I'd gotten enough information. I've discovered about 60 percent I've unearthed was sometimes more than I really wanted to know. After throwing in a large dose of common sense, I'd relax. The rest seemed to come, if I'd wait and be patient, from the Lord Above. I laced my efforts with loads of prayers. Year by year I felt I made real progress in my Leave-It-To-The-Lord-Above effort. I've found, the more I wanted to learn about a subject, the more I would. The more I left to The Lord, the less I worried.

Maybe it was a framed bit of advice from *Elbert Hubbard's Scrapbook,* a gift from my mom, that motivated it.

Keep your mind on the great and splendid thing you want to do. You will find yourself unconsciously seizing the opportunity to fulfill your desire. Everything comes through desire. Every sincere prayer is answered . . .

That's not verbatim. That item is long gone. But not the thought.

After I've availed myself of all the knowledge I can muster on the subject, I try to stop and look around me. Observe other mothers in action in their homes, at church, particularly in public places. I try to be alert, aware of how they handle different situations. I learn from other peoples' experiences and conversations. I'm a professional eavesdropper.

This method caused me to make many vows I didn't know I could keep. But things I knew, I would try to avoid. After supersaturated with how-to's, I looked around. Mostly I decided what kind of a mother I *didn't* want to become. So many didn't seem to enjoy their children and treated them as burdens, not treasures. Some didn't even treat them as people, as they surely are and even talked sweeter to their pets! Here are some types I didn't want to be:

Martyr-to-my-children: Giving them the impression "you're so blessed to have me." Continually telling them they are "children," as if that's a curse instead of a precious time of life; reminding them they are emotionally unstable, ignorant creatures; relating over and over all the things I am denying myself on their account. This is especially damaging when others are present. I cringe at the sight.

The litany goes on to the teen years: Making sure they know how hard you worked to spoil them, never making them work like you had to do, then blessing them out because they don't know how to work. Sure thing when you were growing up, you didn't have a chauffeur. You walked. See, you've forgotten that these trying times were formerly "the good old days," according to who's telling the story. Of course, you don't let the kid know you didn't feel like car pooling today and that you're coming down with a cold. Be sure he knows you're not letting him know by coughing and sneezing. Lots of heavy sighs thrown in.

The martyr complex was apparent in some of the marriages I saw around me. I vowed not to imply: "Now this raising children is full-time, buddy, so bug off. We'll get together again—in a few years. Granted I wanted children. You can overdo anything. You did this to me, you bum, you'll pay. You and your bread, jug of wine, and thou. Look at me now. Fat, broken-down and in trouble."

My conclusions from many years of observing?

I vow to try, with God's help, to convince Chief and my children that they are my blessings of joy, real treasures, not gloom givers.

After I read all the books assembled, sifted through all my observations and eavesdroppings, what then? The enormity of the job of raising children, the awesome task hit me between the eyes. Reality. I'd gotten a little more confident in my homemaker/good bedfellow role. But, all of it can be scary. This was the time I knew I had to master meditation and prayer. No. I didn't have time. I had to *make* time, grab it, steal it, beg and borrow it. Early morning. Late at night. As the children started moving on out, I had more time to meditate and pray easily. I discovered swimming and walking were great for me. Then, when they no longer rode with me, I became prayer-on-wheels.

Why are meditation and prayer so necessary? After all, I had taken time to stop and think, assemble facts, observe. We are not all facade, living only an external life. We are not Humpty Dumpties, mere shells. Nor do we grow, stretch, age, and mature only externally.

We have an *internal* life. Mine needs nurturing, and yours does too. This is where I live. Our bodies are our temples where we invite God Himself to reside. We cultivate His presence. This is where I ask for His help and guidance, strength and courage, where I learn to listen. This is where I find out and constantly seek to know who I am and what He wants me to do, also where He wants me to go. Maybe it is easy for you to find time. Perhaps you can actually hear Him. I listen and listen. I've never heard His voice out loud, only the feeling He approves. I'm jealous of those who do. Maybe if I could move more of me out of the way, I could hear Him. During these life-with-children years, I gave it all I had. I knew I had only one shot at it. A good sense of humor was the oil I needed.

I clung to the fact that there is life after children. I was trying to make sure Chief would be there, too. I thanked God for my responsibilities and my opportunities for personal growth. Even if they were greater, closer together, then I might have desired.

The toughest part of being a mother by far, to me, is setting a good example and putting myself in order. Children learn by example. We're not raising dummies. At least we hope we're not! After all, they have our genes. That's where they got their smarts. Right?

Children are the first to see through us. Examining myself still is the toughest. Assessing my proud's and sorry's.

Example: "I am particular. Just born that way. Come from a long line of perfectionists." Or, "I'm a neatnik. I'm impatient. I'm flighty." Or, "I just have to say what I think. I come from a dynasty of debaters dating back thousands of years. All shakers and movers." Or, "I'm unique. I've always been told that. One of a kind. Not easily lead. Strong but lovable. I really am."

Bert Decker, a psychologist friend, has emphasized we should relax. Don't sweat it. He says, "Twenty-five percent of the people we know will love us regardless. Unconditionally. We can do no wrong; 25 percent don't like us. Can't stand us. Won't buy us, no matter how we present ourselves. The other 50 percent? They're still making up their minds."

There's so much garbage out there in the world: all negative; some downright evil. Influences that call me to carefully reexamine my own personal standards. We're constantly having to be on the lookout, never compromising ourselves, not to be persuaded or moved to do anything we know to be wrong for us in the eyes of God, not man. If I put myself in order and keep myself as near that goal as possible. I've found that's all I can do. That's battle enough, believe me. No phoney self-coercion is necessary, no duty—other than to be myself, hopefully a self acceptable to God.

The duties that accompany mothering, the facts of our assignment, the requirements of our marriage, the necessities of our family sometimes seem more than we can bear.

What someone else tells us we ought to do is not always right to follow. It could be the blind leading the blind. We're not sheep.

We cannot do things that are contrary to our inner selves, our inner values—just because "it's being done *now*. Well, times have changed. In my set, this is it." It's not more "cool" to follow the crowd, as the saying goes, than for "a hummingbird to catch fish because its young are hungry."

Sure you see miserable marriages, churlish children. It's natural to wonder if we can do any better. Don't waste time with self-doubt, self-blame, self-consciousness. With nine children, I never had time to indulge in this pastime. I tried to save all those fears for my quiet time, my meditation time.

Don't worry. That's useless. Worry is just like they say—rocking in a rocker. You're moving, but you're not getting anywhere. Worse yet, when we worry, we're really saying to the Lord, "I don't really believe You're going to take care of me or help me solve these problems." We know He is. His timing might not be our timing, but in His time it will come to pass.

Learning to accept ourselves isn't always easy to do, realizing we can't swap nerves, glands, or brains with our buddies. Can't swap talents and abilities. The good news is—we don't have his/hers limitations or strange mixture of tendencies.

Trying to find and release our own unique capabilities and expressing our own internal value system takes time. You'll see my progress unfold. Using my favorite comparison—a snail on sleeping pills. There was an old song, "It Takes Time." You remember Chief and I hadn't been married anytime when he kept reminding me, which was bad enough, that I couldn't cook like his mother. That's one thing. But to tell any and everyone within earshot was quite a different matter. I had to remind him I was *not* his mother. To make matters worse, the first gift he ever gave me, after marriage, was a sewing machine. She was a super seamstress.

My first Declaration of Independence? Two-score and seven years ago, I declared: "I am *not* your mother. I do not look, think, act, or cook like your mother. No offense. If you don't want to leave your mother, don't. If you insist on clinging to your mother—the door's open. I'd like for you to be the father of my children. I intend to be the best mother to your children I can, with God's help. I plan to work every day, in every way, to make you glad you've married me."

This goes for my sons, too. Nothing gets me more than to hear them say, "Teach my wife to fix squash like you do." Them's fightin' words, Son.

Haven't you seen so many wives try to be a mother to their husband? Everything from dial the phone to packing their clothes. A husband doesn't need a mother. He had one. He needs a helpmate, a soulmate, a playmate, a confidante, a cheerleader, affirmer, and encourager—someone who loves him, "warts and all."

Precious as they are, mothers are no substitutes for wives. Wives are wives. Not mothers of husbands. Besides, no wife wants to be treated like a mother. Sometime she might wish, fleetingly, she were. She wants a husband. She, too, had a mother. Children need a mother. God gave them one—you.

After periodic bouts of assessing who we are—wives, mothers—we learn that it takes a heap of trial and error. Never give up. While you're gathering ammunition for your daily battles, look for the Lord's loving guidance. Don't forget that abundance of humor. You can't have too much.

You're not always born with a good sense of humor. You can work at it. It's easier for some than others. I grew up surrounded with humor. My parents were "characters." Fun to be around. Optimistic. Not doomsday gloomies, just-you-waits, or what-in-the-world-is-the-world-coming-to-s. They laughed aplenty. Smiled most of the time.

If you weren't that blessed, don't despair. Everybody doesn't like that kind of person. They'd rather be around the "let's-see-who-we-can-work-over-today" gang. If it's your desire, you can activate your hidden sense of humor. It's there. You can at least try to cultivate one because you'll need it for survival of your mental, physical, and spiritual health. We're talking about the ability to laugh at ourselves, not making fun of others. That's cruelty, not humor. Teasing can be cruel. I'm talking about learning to see the funny side of the ludicrous, crazy things that happen every day. I had one only last week.

I was in my beach cottage by myself. Writing, of course. I was in an old bathing suit. One of my children called and reported he was coming with a date. His date looks like a model for Ralph Lauren, Bill Blass, or Yves St. Laurent. I tried to get out of my suit into something more presentable. The zipper stuck, wouldn't budge. I thought about calling the construction guys next door. Strangers. I couldn't reach the zipper even if I could locate scissors. Panic.

When my son came, his friend easily unstuck my zipper. In my haste to order pizza for lunch, I discovered to my horror I'd misplaced my money. My son had to pay. After very little indigestion and a whole lot of laughs, I told my plight to the construction guys next door. How I thought about calling them. How I needed them.

To my delight, I discovered they needed me, too. They were standing up in the back of their pickup. One was scrambling on top of the cab. They had discovered a snake. I cooly borrowed their axe and chopped the snake's head off. One went back to work; the other kept his eye on the snake. He didn't even trust a headless one. (To each person, his own panic.)

Funny things happen to us daily if you look for them. Read clean joke books, comics, cartoons. Check out and hang around the good-humored people you know. Observe. Listen. Learn. They draw a crowd, don't they? Are never without friends. The persistently pleasant are the joys of life.

Heaven save us from The Great Pretenders. The "heavies." The pompously self-righteous. The self-important peacocks. Even if they are do-gooders, they give a bad name to goodness. It's not what you do but how you do it that puts those around you at ease.

Now we've checked ourselves and set our priorities—not someone else's ideas of what our priorities should be. We're off to battle. We're gonna tree 'em with a grin. We're ready for the Juggling Jester role.

The Juggling Jester is one who can learn the hang of cooking with one hand, listening to homework with one ear, and piano practice with the other, simultaneously, and with a Jester's demeanor. How?

Maybe you're a genius and can think about four things at once. (Remember, we learned to accept ourselves with our limitations.) I can do four things at once but not very well. With nine, I had to, but I can't *think* about four things at once. Maybe you can. Maybe you can remember to pick up the dry cleaning, take the baby for his shot, bake cookies for the sale, all between piano lessons and football practice.

Not me. From day one—childhood—I've been a listmaker. A confirmed packrat, I still run across sketches I made for a dress I designed for my mom to make, a list of accessories I needed, not to mention important papers due. I have always been into booklets. I'm the answer to an office-supply company's dream. Although I wasn't a secretary, I was a billing clerk a year before marriage. My dream is to *have* a secretary.

I've filled more than my share of notebooks for my own personal use. Throughout my life, I've been into diaries, lists, and journals of all kinds. If you're missing your club minutes, I've probably got them in their eternal resting place, my attic.

Journals of all kinds are poked around my house. My number-one book is *Journal of Ideas,* sometimes clothes, decorating, or thumbnail sketches to be enlarged into a watercolor later. Or ideas for a short story. I sketch a light bulb by it. Then when I have time I transfer it to my idea notebook, which has a light bulb on the front.

Number-two is my *Learn Something Every Day* book. How ambitious can you get? There I jot down anything of interest to me, whether I learned it from my reading, television, or eavesdropping. On days I have no entry, I pick up the encyclopedia, the dictionary, or the Bible. Goethe wrote, "Daring ideas are like chessmen moved forward. They may be beaten, but they may start a winning game." You've no idea how handy these journals have been to me over the years.

Number-three is a little booklet I always keep in my purse in case I get an idea while I'm out. Number-four is one by my bed for words I need to look up. Number-five is *Think.* I write down anything that pops into my mind in a rough-and-tumble manner. Sometimes the writing cools—especially while driving. I can hardly read it. Number-six is another booklet I keep bedside for ideas I might have during the night. Sometimes it's difficult to read when I write in the dark. (A friend gave me a pen with a light, but the battery's always going dead.) Number-seven book is another supposedly stay-in-place kind by the telephone. It's common property and harder to keep up with. Here messages or any info received via telephone is supposed to be recorded. Number-eight I've labeled *Let's Be Entertaining.* It's notebook sized. Any entertaining I do, large or small, goes into this book: who my guests are, plus members of the family. I have to have a head count starting with Chief and me. Always forget to include us somehow. Here I record my guests' likes and dislikes, what I fed them last, recipes I've culled from my cookbook collection that I want to serve. I write them on the page. (I'm so messy, I'd ruin the cookbook.)

Since I had such a big brood to begin with, we don't feel like it's a party unless we have at least two dozen. So, beside the regular recipes, I write the calculated, multiplied proportions for my dinner party.

I plan the event from the time the guests hit the door until they leave. With themes usually. I record not only what I fed them (so I wouldn't repeat it next time they come), but note my Proud's and Sorry's. Such as—"best I pick up a simple flower arrangement next time. Not my talent. Everything jumped out of the vase at me." Or, "fixed far too much" or "too little of that." Proud's & Sorry's include "that dish most enjoyed" or "none of this seemed to go over."

This method's not to count. "We've had them four times to their once." It's just to help me release my brain from overload.

By far the most important book I kept when all nine were home was book number nine. The troops dubbed it *My Brain*. It was notebook size. All I had to do was ask them to fetch *My Brain*, and they knew exactly what I meant. They knew if it got lost I'd never make it. If for any reason I was incapacitated, someone could carry on. Keep the family afloat on schedule.

Every night before I went to bed I whipped out *My Brain* and made my next-day lists. I prefer the Must-Do, Should-do, If-Time-To, and so forth method. The Must-Do was a string of things. (I enjoy getting some of the oldie *Brains* out to remember when all nine were home.) The Must-Do was full of doctor's appointments, music lessons, Scouts, all kinds of ballgames and practices.

Should-Do usually was the next column: "Drop off lamp to be repaired, take dry cleaning" sort of things. If-Have-Time unfortunately included "Write Mom, write Sally." Like-To-Do was "start knitting Jeter's sweater. Practice my backswing. Do my nails. Plan what to wear Saturday night. Or finish article I started writing."

Another column was Meal Plans. Done in meeting with designated child from the Chore Chart. (I explained that in detail in *The Pains and Pleasures of Parenthood.*) This child and I checked the deep freeze, pantry, and fridge to make sure there were no missing items needed to complete the meal plans. There was always an ever-running grocery list posted near the fridge.

On this same page of *My Brain* I added the rough-and-tumble pocket-book notes, the telephone list, those needs of the troops and those Chief gave me. I had to put them in some sort of order. More importantly, I not only had to schedule what I had to do but to route myself so I wouldn't be running around in circles, driving needless miles. I wasn't working for the Big-wheel award. (People who go around in circles are known as Big Wheels.)

For example, I'd drop off clothes at the cleaners on the way to a class. While at class, I could do needlework, read, or visit with other mothers. I usually brought happiness, either by coming or going. As I'd hear them whisper, "At least I don't have nine children." Little did they know how I loved it . . . and hoped it showed. On pretty days, I'd take the preschoolers walking or to the library. The older ones could practice unnoticed.

Businesses are organized, filled with little details, have filing systems, in-and-out lists, schedules. The in-and-out list came in handy when the kids were teenagers.

The Jesting Juggler was busy. Sandwiched in between their needs I found little islands of time for me and for Chief. Most important, sometimes in weird hours or weird places that made these moments together even more precious.

How busy is busy?

3

Chief's Balancing Act:
Surviving Forty-two Years
of College Tuitions

Some men wonder how they could live without women. The answer is: *cheaper*. Chief declares it's a very expensive way of getting his laundry done free.

Still using the Peter-Paul principle, testing "for richer or poorer," Chief has had reasons to stop and think. If "advertising" can be accused of persuading people to live beyond their means, so can matrimony. With a wife and nine children, Chief has had to put up with a lot of persuaders.

Fortunately, I grew up in the era when females were not expected to work outside the home. Certainly there were exceptions. Chief's father and I often discussed "working women". North Carolina led the nation in the highest number of working women. With two tobacco companies, our town was number-one in the state. Since Chief's father worked in the office of one, he had chances to observe this new phenomenon. A daddy who was trying to support his family during the Great Depression, he had strong views.

Chief's father believed women in the workplace were really taking a man's place. In his estimation, marriages and mothering suffered. So to this day, Chief and I have our differences of opinion. Two views of the same thing. We're not talking about "having to work." We're talking about choices of working outside the home. Courtship makes a man spoon, but matrimony makes him fork over.

"Does Elizabeth work?"

All my older relatives called me Elizabeth. If reprimanded, it was Emily Elizabeth.

"What do you mean, 'Does Elizabeth work?' "

"You know, *all* women today are supposed to work."

Two aunts were "discussing" me at a family reunion. Deafness runs in our family. Comes in handy. My family always thought I had the nicest, quietest, well-behaved children. I was amused they thought I couldn't hear them. Thought they were whispering.

'No . . . Elizabeth doesn't work." One aunt yelled to the other. "She doesn't *have* to. *She married well!*"

In my talks, I tell 'em all, "I don't *go* to work, I'm *surrounded* by it." I also tell those other women at home to be sure to give their spouse a big hug. Be sure to thank them for working, telling them how grateful you are for having "married well."

There are more ways than one to say "I love you." Going to work is one of them. Chief is most generous. If I ask for one, remember, I get four. We named six children before they were born, and thanks be to God, have nine. So if I press the issue. "Do you love me?" he always says, "Here's my checkbook. Check the stubs!"

You'd be touched to know that Chief, once during our courting days, said, "I bet you wouldn't marry me, Libbylove." I not only called his bet but raised him nine.

Luckily for Chief, we had only two daughters. We Griffin females often wished the same spirit of generosity had prevailed with shoes as it did okra. I told Chief once I needed "a tad" of okra for some soup. He brought home a peck. Do you know how much a *peck* of okra is? You don't want to, believe me. It's taken me twenty years to enjoy okra again.

What man hasn't stumped his wife with the question, "Why do you need a pair of shoes? You have a pair!"?

Like Imelda Marcos, we had to sneak our new shoes in like contraband. I really felt sorry for Imelda. The whole world had to know how many pairs she had.

We girls could get real emotional about our fashion needs. Chief was unimpressed. Dubbed us "oceans of emotions surrounded by expanses of expenses," so as soon as our daughters could work outside Bedlam (what we called our home) they did. Chief was pleased. He considered their buying their own clothes like he did the boys' expenditures. "Everybody has to support their own vices."

Chief is still asked so many times "how he supported" all of us—carefully and prayerfully. Now a word from management—Chief—recorded by labor—Libbylove:

"Our children know that God is the Great Provider. God gives every bird its food. But He does *not* throw it into the nest.

"Children cut grass or baby-sat as they came of age. Then at age sixteen, if not participating in high-school sports, they were expected to get parttime jobs. Three of them had over three-thousand dollars in the bank when they graduated from high school.

"I expected my children to have enough money to pay their first-semester tuition and fees for college. Because I believe in letting them invest their money first, for their education for the first year.

"If they spent their hard-earned money first, we'd be assured they wanted to go to college. They wanted an education. After that I would invest my money next. (We had two at the same time in college for eighteen years; four in college for three years; three in college for four years.)

"During this particular period, I realized that from a safety stand-point, it was better for my children to drive their own cars. We didn't give them new cars. They had used vehicles, usually our handmedowns which would do the job.

"For several years we had eight cars on our insurance program! We were very fortunate: no auto accidents or speeding tickets. We never had to bail 'em out of jail.

"Later on, I lent four of them money for down payments on their homes. I don't believe in renting. I want them to own their own homes. They could make monthly payments, but they didn't have down pay-ments. I told them this was only a *loan*, Not a gift. I expected them to pay me back." 'Daddy, what happens if I don't pay you back?'

'I have another way of collecting it.'

'How?'

'Libbylove and I will come live with you.'

"So far, so good.

"I've had the privilege of setting up one of our sons in two businesses by making loans for him. Libbylove and I are financially involved with each of our nine to some extent.

"Three of the older marrieds wanted a beach cottage. I went with them and bought a place. It's now worth four times what it was when purchased in 1972.

"We had our own time-sharing program before they became popular. But at least it was family-owned. The time sharing therefore could be altered to our own needs.

"In my dental office, I show that I believed in the American free-enterprise system. To that extent in 1965, I instituted an incentive plan. I pay a weekly salary to my office personnel, plus a monthly bonus plan, based on the gross income that we generated.

"I've never had much money. Never wanted much money. I'd never thought about having a big family, but for those of you who live on a shoestring, here are some things I learned:

"From the standpoint of a private investor, over the period of years, I learned that five-thousand dollars was a magic number.

"Several times I was able to invest five-thousand dollars with several other people to put up a certain amount whereby we could purchase property or apartments which generated a nice income after a period of years.

"These ideas might help you small investors. I've been involved in two-fold situations saving a hundred dollars a month until I had five-thousand dollars to invest. Then on a smaller scale, I was in an investment club which put in twenty-five dollars a month and bought stock which turned out to be worth over twelve-thousand dollars after a period of years. After we disbanded, I was able to invest that money into a real estate project which generated a very nice return. When self-employed, one has to put money aside in a retirement fund or it won't be there.

"I've always been one who believed in life insurance, especially whole life. As a young person it takes many years to build up a cash-value reserve. Later, I was able to borrow on my cash reserve and make several investments at a cheaper interest rate than your routine bank loan. Therefore, life insurance is a two-fold investment. Cash value plus protection.

"Once in 1972, I borrowed five-thousand dollars on my life insurance at 5 percent and bought a four-unit apartment house. I gave half interest to number-one son, who managed it. Ten years later we sold it. Each one of us made seventeen-thousand dollars on the deal.

"We invested ten-thousand dollars of that each in another real estate development and over a period of six years received a twenty-eight-thousand-dollar return.

"This just shows that a small investment can give a good return on your money if done wisely.

"I'm talking about average people making it in the financial world. I think one should always save 10 percent of their income. Whether invested in a home, real estate, or life insurance, whereby you may have more to invest later in life at a minimum of interest.

"Since I was a dentist, and in a service field, my philosophy in earning an income was to render a service at a reasonable fee. And the income took care of itself.

"We had always planned to have a large family, if the Good Lord would bless us with children. We named six children before we were married and allowed to have nine blessings. Therefore money was not my God.

"We did not send our children to church, as Libbylove told you in *The Pains and Pleasures of Parenthood*. We took them with us. We believed that if one is exposed to the teachings of Christ, they may deviate at one time, but chances are they'll come back because they've been taught the right way of living.

"I have been blessed with most of my patients paying me what they owe me. However, I had one that I had to personally call on to collect.

" 'Well, did a personal call do any good?' Libbylove asked. 'Did he pay you?'

" 'Not only he didn't pay me, he had the nerve to gnash at me with *my* teeth!'

"Progress always involves risk. You can't steal second base and keep one foot on first.

"I'm proud of my children, proud of their leadership abilities. Leaders first, then second, they are able to persuade others to go with them.

"Big shots are only small shots that keep on shooting.

"Progress of a great man: quits sharing his own ideas; quits writing his own letters; quits writing his own speeches.

"What this country needs is cleaner minds and dirtier fingernails.

"Reputation? Make ten consecutive guesses, and you're an established expert—until you make one little mistake.

"Yes, I am a 'self-made man.' And Libbylove reminds me I relieved the Lord of a great responsibility."

4

The Disappearing Act: Cutting the Apron Strings

School days are the best days of your life, if your children are old enough to go. School days are the worst days of your life, when your children are leaving for college.

No one prepared me for this moving-out day. I remember the joy I felt when the first child entered the first grade. Kindergarten under her belt, an enjoyable experience, she was excited about first grade. I was excited for her.

Why aren't I excited today? She's leaving for college. Haven't I always laughingly declared that checkout time at Bedlam was eighteen? She's right on target.

Growing up is what every teen looks forward to, especially flying the coop. The dear Lord, Master of Timing, knows it's mutual, when you have four teens at one whack. Going to college was a natural, progressive step. All these things I told myself.

But this was my number-one child. Eighteen years of joy. A beautiful girl. Of course there's only one beautiful/handsome child and every mother has him or her. My daughter was no exception. After Bedlam, college would be a retreat for her. She was cool, calm, and collected. Born that way. Proper, like my mom, thank goodness.

So who was I fooling? Not the dear Lord. He knew how I hated to see her go. I didn't want to make an outward show of my inner feelings. I wanted her to know the excitement and anticipation I shared for her. I felt like saying something stupid like, "Don't you want to take a year off, kid? Kinda take it easy? Hang around?"

This is what my mom said to me. The difference? It was after my college graduation, not high school. I was the youngest. At the time, I thought that was about the most ridiculous idea my usually sensible mom ever had. Now I knew the feeling.

I did question the wisdom of my daughter going to my alma mater. That was her choice. I mumbled something about how hard it was academically. A ridiculous remark! My number-one child was much smarter and made better grades than I.

Like my own mom, I sent a trunkful of clothes with her, like she'd never have any again. The clothes that make a woman break a man. I figured she'd never have that many again.

Curbing my nostalgia was my biggest problem, helping her get settled into her dorm. The old school hadn't changed all that much. I gave her reassuring, affirming messages. I curbed my "You know what to do and what not to do." I took her with a smile. I left her with a smile.

Once home, it was a different story. I took time for tears alone. I missed her so much I wouldn't go into her room for months. After all, she was my Miss Dependable, my right hand—a treasure. Just think, as I often do, if she hadn't been such a satisfactory child, my childbearing days might have ended then and there. Think what I would have missed.

As each one left the nest, I dwelt on the great contribution that child had made to our brood. Being the oldest, she had stood by me all these years. The little mother. The official worrier. How could I let her go? Who'd I talk girl talk with? We females were so outnumbered. Shared interests in clothes, books, swimming, the beach, and sporting events. Mainly laughs. We giggled together. Thanks be to God, I had another girl coming along to keep me company.

The apron strings were cut.

Number one was leaving the nest. I knew it would never be the same. It wasn't. It never got any easier. One by one every two or three years I knew they'd be leaving. Each one left a void. Not like Eddie. Remember Eddie? "Eddie doesn't live here anymore."

"Do you have anyone to fill the vacancy?"

"Nope. Eddie didn't leave any vacancy."

Did I worry about my daughter? Or my sons that soon followed suit? No. If I hadn't said it by now, taught them by now, it was far too late.

No, I know they have all the tools, the coping mechanisms, within themselves. God's armor of protection. They've been taught right from wrong. I had done all I could. They are no longer children. Fantastic young folks. I hated to see them go. When you pamper, you hamper. They could fly on their own. I knew they could go as far as the Lord intended.

I lost some splendid chauffeurs. When we lived in town at Trinity Treat, they were within walking distance of school. Living at Bedlam was a different story. One of the youngsters constantly asked to be driven some place. One day I was so tired I thought I was talking to my driving-age ones. I asked, "What do you think God gave you two legs for?"

"One for the brake and one for the gas."

Looking at a miserable fifteen-year-old boy, I understood. Walking is the pits.

I really got a ribbing when I took the oldest son to college.

"Hey, Charlie, did your mom take you to college?" One of Chief's golfing buddies asked another. (I met Chief after his golf game to tell him all about this great day.)

"Naw. I had to catch a train and haul the trunk up those dorm stairs."

The foursome laughed. That's okay. Trains don't run through our town anymore. Besides, I wanted to take my son. I like to know what their dorm rooms look like. I like to know where they put their heads at night. So when I say my prayers for them every night, I can envision their snuggling in their beds. In college? Dream on.

Sitting around talking with a bunch of dental wives at a meeting, one mentioned she was in the admissions office of a nearby school.

"Do you know of a school that takes average students? I have a son who's not super smart or super athletic. Just a super boy. One of the best."

"That's just the kind of student we're looking for," my friend replied. "We want students we don't have to bail out of jail. That have a sense of responsibility. Sounds like yours fits the bill. We're looking for good folks."

"You've got it. A great guy."

This was the sizzling sixties. The males had to wear shirt and tie for dinner. What a ludicrous sight! Guys with shirt and tie over a pair of shorts. These were the casual college days, where they didn't exactly drink at the fountain of knowledge. They just sort of gargled a little.

Our son changed our way of thinking about a lot of things. He finished college in four years with above-average grades. He changed Chief's theory of no cars on campus. It only took one recounting of a horrendous ride home our son had from college. The driver had discovered that college is a fountain where all go to drink. He was doing all he could for his thirst.

Thereafter each son inherited one of our hand-me-down cars. We trusted their driving far more. You learn with each child. We learned about telephones. Anyone who thinks television has destroyed conversation doesn't have to pay the phone bill after your boys discover girls, especially out-of-towners. Always the best kind, of course. Aren't we parents foolish? We spend the first three years of a child's life trying to get 'em to talk—and the next eighteen trying to get them to shut up.

College is a tough adjustment for some. They discover it's a place where the person who picks up after you is *you*. Not true in my case. I was outnumbered. They picked up after themselves. Cause and effect still reigned. You made the mess—you picked it up.

I almost allowed myself to get caught up in the care-packages-from-home routine. I couldn't wait to send number-one child, away from home, something to eat. I remembered my college days and cafeteria food. My mom wasn't into pampering. But I recalled my feelings when I saw others receive packages from home. Envy. So I made up a box of food with tins of homemade fudge. I had finally mastered fudge, thanks to friend Maggie's recipe. For thirty years I turned out chocolate that ranged from runny to scorched.

What delight I used to take in sending care packages to Chief during his dental-school days, especially chock full of his favorite candy bars.

What ended my care-package days?

When I went to pick my daughter up for Christmas holidays, I spied my tins still filled with the fudge, untouched, molded. "Bad for your complexion. Calories," she said. I never attempted anything that foolish again except once, when some fraternity was raising money for charity. They were sending care exam packages to lucky students. I fell for it. They never received their packages. It didn't matter with number-one son, he soon had a "route" taking orders and delivering snacks for his dorm buddies. That, with his laundry route, like his father Chief's school days, kept him in spending money.

Fortunately for me, especially for the provider, Chief, there was a little lull between shipping out to college. Children were still shaping up at home, still growing, stretching, learning. I was learning, too. Here's one idea that made my *Idea Book*. If you become concerned because you haven't heard from your youngsters who are away from home, at camp or college, just send the child your usual letter, but add a postscript something like this: "Hope you can use this ten dollars I'm enclosing." *Then don't enclose it!* The boy or girl may not have written home for a long time, but that P.S. will bring a letter in a flash. Count on them to add their own little concerned P.S.: "I didn't find the ten dollars you mentioned."

Chief and I believe in continuing education. You better believe educating nine children is *continuing* education. In fact, Chief paid for forty-two years of college tuitions before the last one threw in his sheepskin. I say he definitely suffers from mal-tuition.

During these short breathing spells, financially, between the disappearing acts and college days, there was business at home as usual. The first two who left the nest rarely came home for weekends. Our oldest, a daughter, went to a school that didn't allow freshmen to come home until Christmas. Same rule when I was there. Smart. Who'd come back? Some didn't. I loved it. (I'd discovered art, fanning the flame lit by my high-school art teacher. Totally in love with the subject, I was one of the first graduates in this new major—one of seven.)

Child number two, the son, didn't come home weekends. He was into heavy-duty courting. His true love lived across the state. She was in nursing school. So he was my first road runner. 'Tis said that boys who whine grow up to be "groan" men. He didn't whine for gas money. He got it the old-fashioned way. He earned it. The rule, "You pay for your own vices," held. In my streams of "Keep them safe, Dear Lord," he headed the list that four years.

"Every time I think about your driving on the highway weekends, I get another gray hair," brought no comments from my kids. They knew I came from a long line of premature, fullheaded, whiteheaded people. Only one of mom's six had no gray hairs—a sister, who never confessed until it was too late for the rest of us, that she had secretly munched Brewer's Yeast all those years. I never mentioned my gray hair again. I knew better. I'd get the same response, "Oh, so you're the one who gave Grandma her white hair?"

I was so busy with seven still at home, I didn't think about why the two college kids never brought anyone home. Truth is, Bedlam could have been too crowded. I kept telling them what they call "congestion" in Bedlam would be called "intimate" someplace else. Maybe they felt like they did when they were my built-in babysitters. When I'd be a little late returning than I anticipated, I'd apologize. Their standard, good-humored acceptance speech was, "Don't apologize. I wouldn't be in a hurry to come home either."

Maybe they never knew what they'd find. Number-one son did bring a college friend by the house one Friday afternoon. I was doing a dress rehearsal for an upcoming Saturday night costume party. I had been next door to elicit my good neighbor's approval. I got it. Not my son's. You can imagine his embarrassment to have to introduce this silver-clad-all-over female as his mother!

Those kids left behind couldn't wait to spread out their sleeping quarters. Luxuriate in more space. As they left the Bedlam boundaries to take baby-sitting, grass-cutting, and store-clerking jobs, there were always others waiting to inherit their car window. So they knew there was a line behind them, as well as support. Each always had their own bed and chest of drawers but rarely their own room.

Those in college didn't completely forget those at home. Here's a poem that was sent me. The author, as often was the case, did not sign her name. Whoever thought it might be included in a book someday?

Advice from a Daughter Off to College

So long, dearest Mother.
Your fledgling has flown.
Now please do be careful
While you're on your own.
Discard that blue dress—it's no longer your size.
And it really would help if you made up your eyes.
Don't twist at parties—at your age, it's square.
But you might take a fling at teasing your hair.
Do let's chuck out that vile pea-green rug.
And Pete is fourteen: he's too big to bug.
I'll write to you often. Kindly resist
Trying to figure the boys I have kissed.
Keep Dad on the beam. Keep Pete from my room.
Keep the home fires burning. Don't melt in gloom.
I'll be home for Thanksgiving, and it will be nice
To listen again on all *your* advice.

—Author Unknown

Yes, those away were beginning to mother me. Those at home had to be loved still, nurtured, taught, and disciplined by me.

Bedlam hadn't changed all that much. The messages move up and down the ranks in a big family. News travels. Even teenagers respect authority. Discipline, they sense, is a special kind of attention. Without it, love and respect fly out the window. "If you don't respect your own rights, you may neglect the rights of others."

The Jesting Juggler, me, still sought to find the fine line between showing too much concern and too little, being too strict and too lenient, knowing when to hold tight and when to let go.

My letting-go adjustments never became any easier. When my third child was ready to leave for college, again I thought I couldn't bear it. This child was my peacemaker, a born mediator.

The first son was a live wire, energetic, outspoken disciplinarian. Outspoken by few. The younger ones knew he was the man in charge when he baby-sat them. They became his "go-fers." Yet none of the older children enjoyed the arrival of a newborn any more than he did. He always put his stamp of approval on them, claiming that the latest one was "the cutest one yet, Mom." He admitted I was getting good at it.

Son number two, child number three, was a most important cog in the family wheel. Babies didn't interest him like the preschoolers. They followed him around like the Pied Piper. People lover, as gregarious as one can be, he could draw a crowd. With the first two gone, the problem with number three gone meant number four was just one year behind.

When it was time for us to take number three, there was much wailing from the younger ones. Peacemakers are hard to come by. I didn't feel too happy about his leaving either. Chief went with me to take number three. The school of his choice was a two-year Baptist junior college. It wasn't close by like the others.

The sight of my son standing on that big front porch all by himself is forever etched in my memory. He was to share a room at a rooming house in the little town. He was the first arrival. No other students had shown up yet. If his little childhood sweetheart hadn't gone with us, I might not have made it.

Again, I never wanted them to see me cry good-byes. I prefer smiles and see-you-laters. Can't stand prolonged good-byes.

Chief, the wedding weeper, will cry with you—a bucketful. I always figured someone had to keep their wits. Again, I'm a private crybaby. Maybe it's my hotel background. Hello and good-bye were constants.

Like number-one son, number three was also into heavy courting. The difference? Number-three's girlfriend lived in the same town we lived in and was going to school there. So the suitcase-college era was launched at Bedlam. Those next three brought friends home most weekends, to my delight.

A few years ago, I had an unexpected pleasure. One of number-three son's buddies introduced me when I gave a talk. I enjoyed hearing his version of visiting Bedlam: Friday night late arrival was normal for this college crew. Chief was already asleep. Moms never sleep, so I was the greeter.

Next morning, the college crew slept in. By the time they came down for one of my big show-off breakfasts, Chief had gone golfing. *The usual*

Saturday morning confusion was a minimum, I thought. The little ones enjoyed hanging around sophisticated college kids as much as I did.

What fun we had making signs, posting notes of welcome around Bedlam. Don said that in the middle of breakfast, a man came into the kitchen and helped himself to a cup of coffee. I walked in. We chatted as he checked the fridge. He took some things out. Went back outside and brought back a case of milk. He rearranged the bottles and the things he had put on the counters beside the milk. He poured himself another cup of coffee. I walked to the door with the man. All the while we were talking and commenting on the upcoming football game.

While we were outside, Don asked number three if this man helping himself to coffee was "Chief." He had never met him.

"No," my son laughed, the rest of the crew joining in, "That's the milkman!"

The next two sons went to the same college. Each left a void. Number-four son was another live wire like son number one. Teasing was his favorite indoor sport. To try to upset my equanimity was his delight. He was very communicative. His skills were both written and verbal. Sons one and two played football and number-three son was a sportswriter for the high school newspaper. He probably would have had more opportunity to develop his sports-oriented talents, but he was the "Mono Kid." Although he had been voted the most improved basketball player for his team, this debilitating teenage pest zapped him.

Once was enough. He took the first bout with mononucleosis real well. The second time around was another story. The first time, he was depressed. He didn't want me out of his sight. The second time, he was enraged. He didn't want me in his sight. I understood his frustrations. Humor, again, was a relief. One of his friends put posters on both ends of the street: "Please go visit Ted. He has mono." His "Have you visited Ted lately?" signs relieved the pressure of living with a caged tiger with a thorn in his paw.

We had our share of sickness and broken bones in Bedlam. As usual, we thanked God it wasn't any worse.

We had another three-year stretch before we took number five to college. It never got any easier. We loved having them home. No hurry, don't rush them. There were still survival skills, social skills, rocks to build lives on, to be taught. Balance was sought in the mental, physical, spiritual realms.

The hardest part? As always, to live your faith and beliefs. The verbal is there but does no good if you say one thing and do another.

We learned plenty about the changes in colleges and education since we graduated. The type of education a student receives sometimes depends on the type of institution he attends—educational or coeducational. We've learned the faculty really are the people who get what's left after the football coach receives his salary. And our kids graduated from college and not a dollar too soon. The last one finished four years and our bank account. His letters: "Dear Chief, haven't heard from you in weeks. Send me a check so I'll know you're all right."

5

When the Fur Flew:
We're Anything but Dull

"I don't know why in the world you want to date *him*," Chief's mom declared. "He has the worst temper."

To say I was shocked would be putting it mildly. I had just met the woman. Chief and I had dated only a few times. We had just popped in for him to pick up something, and I was standing in the middle of the entryway, waiting alone. The area to my right looked like a living room. It was empty. The area to my left looked like a music room. I saw a man sitting down holding a little boy.

His mom appeared from somewhere with this sudden pronouncement, like Moses with a tablet of truth that had to be told, whether you wanted to hear it or not.

Before I had a chance to blink, Chief reappeared. His mom was nowhere around. I felt awkward. Chief disappeared again. I looked to the left at the older man and decided to walk into the room.

"Please don't get up," I insisted, as he tried to balance book and child. "I don't want to interrupt your story."

"Oh, we're just looking at pictures," he smiled. "This is my grandson."

"I'm a friend of Kimball's . . . Libbylove . . . he calls me 'Lib.' "

The man nodded pleasantly. Just then Chief reappeared, beckoning me to come on.

Once outside I asked, "Was that your father, by chance, I saw in the living room?" Trying not to show my irritation. Chief nodded affirmatively.

"Why didn't you introduce him to me?"

"It looked like you'd met him." Chief replied, pleasantly testy.

We rode down the road in silence. I felt comfortable with him. Comfortable when he was a talking machine. I had to steal a glance. *Temper? He's an absolute charmer. Besides, what do I care? He's just a friend, a fun friend at that.*

I was fifteen, soon to turn sixteen. I dismissed with humor Chief's mom's assessment of his disposition. *Maybe she looks on me as a threat— "after" her son. Some moms look on every female as a predator. What a joke. Her son's fun to be with. True, but his manners are questionable. Husband material? No way. Playmate? The best.*

What does a sixteen-year-old know about mate selection? That was one of the first common bonds Chief and I shared. "Give me space." I didn't want to go steady. He didn't want to go steady. So we dated each other in defense, too young to realize we were "going steady." Just friends.

This denial lasted through high school and two years into college on my part. It wasn't until he left to go away to dental school did I realize it must be love.

"You usually have the most bubbly disposition," my mom observed with a smile. "You are either irritable or in another world. I don't know which is worse." She took me by the shoulders, looking into my eyes. "I'll be so glad when Kimball Griffin's here again. I can't stand you when he's gone."

"Mom," I tried to manage a laugh, "I'm not that bad, am I?"

She nodded.

"What in the world's the matter with me? I haven't felt like this since I got so homesick at camp!"

"You're in love."

"*Love?*"

She nodded again.

"Love? I can't be in love. I'm miserable. Simply miserable."

Mom kept nodding and smiling sympathetically.

"I thought you were supposed to be happy. Deliriously happy. I'm miserable!"

"Misery's just a state of mind. A condition. Think. Are you more miserable *with* him or *without* him?"

"Oh, much more miserable *without* him. It's no fun without him."

"That's love, Libbylove." She grinned and hugged me.

"Get out your yardstick before it's too late," she continued.

"What do you mean?"

"Has he told you he loves you?"

"Well," I hedged, ". . . not in so many words. No."

"But he must. He surely spends a lot of time hanging around here. I think he loves you."

"I admit I find him a delight. Enthusiastic. Energetic. Not afraid of hard work. Ambitious. Verbal. Outgoing."

"I agree," Mom said. "I trust you with him . . ." she hesitated. "I guess, best of all, he seems to listen to me. We all like that," she laughed. "He has all the qualities that count. Besides, he adores you. I see it in his eyes. Even if he doesn't say it." She got serious. "What are your reservations?"

"Oh, Mom. He's so full of blarney. Then baloney, when he overdoes his talking. Not like any of the many lines I've heard males throw. I never have that secure feeling. Or, know if he's teasing or serious. I want to say, 'Will the real Kimball please stand up?' That's what one part of me says. Then, I think about manners. Consideration. He has to have his way." I jumped up. "Can you believe he has the ability to make me feel responsible if the movie's lousy. I had nothing to do with it. Made in Hollywood. And remember what his mom said about his temper?"

"Temper? Calm down yourself."

I sat back down.

"Listen to me. If I'm wrong, correct me." I nodded. "You never felt strongly about those other guys. With manners. Showering you with compliments. Gifts. Even poems. You tired of it." I nodded. "You told me that's one of the things you liked about him. He didn't smother you. Gave you space. It's your problem if you allow him to make you feel responsible for a sorry movie. You didn't like the others because you always had your way. You found it boring. Has to have his way? That's a man." Mom continued. "Part of the authority figure. You wouldn't want a mealymouth. (A wimp, they call them today.) You draw the line very clearly. Not way out there." She gestured. "But right close to what you'll put up with and what you will not put up with. He'll abide by it. Love and respect you for it. He's a good man."

"About his temper?"

"I've never seen it. Have you?"

"No."

"Why don't you leave well enough alone?" Mom looked me straight in the eye. "Unless you think you'd better test it. Maybe his mom knows something we don't."

So I did test it. After all, he had tested me, a game player. Instead of asking, "Will you go steady with me?" or "I want you to be *my* girl," much less "I love you" or "Hope you'll marry me someday," he has his own ways.

He just didn't show up one Sunday.

He worked Friday and Saturday nights, so we usually dated most Sunday afternoons and every Sunday night. I dated different boys the other nights. He had been coming around regularly Sundays. I left that day open in case. After all, we had a pact not to go steady with anyone, even each other.

Not being a mind reader, I falsely assumed to read his mind. A real no-no. I assumed he was coming. He usually did.

Some guys dropped by my house this particular Sunday afternoon with their customary comment, "Just checking." The practice was called "checking." Boys went in groups, for protection, I guess. They'd check by girls' houses. If they found someone at home, they'd stay and chat, particularly if the mother provided good snack food. Then they checked out to another's house. If two groups met at the same house, they usually ignored the girl and talked to each other about sports. She loved seeing them, being with them, hearing them. She liked to be checked.

"Where's Dynamite?" they asked. (Chief's nickname: 136 pounds of dynamite. He played blocking back on our high-school football team).

"Haven't seen him," I replied.

"He'll probably show up later."

I nodded.

"There's one in every crowd." I looked at the guy, dying to tell me something. I didn't bite. I don't play games. When I didn't take that bait, he added, "I saw him through the window. He's at _____'s house."

I was stunned. _____ had an unsavory reputation, deserved or not.

"I don't believe it," I countered. I didn't like some of the guys he ran around with. Thought they'd be bad influences. But girls. I'd never known him to pay any attention to any but those seemingly "the best." I continued, "He has a right to date or check any girl he chooses. But I bet it was a look-alike. I doubt if it was _____."

Sensing my indignation, they amiably but defensively challenged me, "Come on walking with us. It's not far. We'll show you."

There were no telltale cars in those days. If a guy wanted to see you bad enough, he walked. You, in turn, appreciated the effort.

_____'s house was close to the street. Through the open window, I could see Chief's unmistakeable profile. One glimpse was enough for me. I was terrified he would see me.

"Let's go," I whispered to my friends as we strolled out of sight of the house. "What's it to me? We had no date. I wasn't stood up. I'm just disappointed . . ." My voice trailed off. ". . . Forget it. Free country." I brightened.

"Come on, walk with us to the drugstore. We love to be seen with a beautiful girl." I smiled in appreciation.

That evening, after supper, Chief appeared. I was ready. I had a school picture of his we had exchanged. His football letter he wanted me to "keep" for him. I was sitting on the front porch. He came grinning, as usual. He walked up the steps. I didn't get up, greet him, or ask him in, as I normally would.

I just gave him my drop-dead look and said, "I hope you've enjoyed dating me."

He kept grinning.

". . . because you've had your last date with me."

He just kept grinning. "I didn't have a date with you . . . you date others."

"I don't date guys with questionable reputations." I hesitated. ". . . if I know it." I paused. "When you date _____, you're putting me on her level."

"I had to teach you a lesson." He kept on, with that silly grin on his face. "I had to let you know how it feels.

"Feels?"

"How it feels to me to have you date others. So I had to use an extreme move."

"You did?" He was looking serious for a change. Was he baiting me? Still playing games? "Sure, I date others. What is it to you? I didn't think you cared. You've never said you did."

"Didn't it ever occur to you I did?"

"No. Didn't it ever occur to you that all you had to do was say, 'Hey, let's go steady,' or words to that effect. Or 'I want you to be just my girl?' For a guy that talks all the time, you can say the least. Quit playing games!"

"I didn't think you cared."

Again, no commitment, no words. One moment I had to be a mind reader. Next, I could read him like a book. I could read him. He cared. He wanted to drive me to make the commitment. No way.

"Guess I'll have to kiss you," he teased. That devilish grin again.

"Oh," I countered. "Don't do me any favors. You're not doing a thing, remember, plenty of guys wouldn't be glad to do for you."

"Since you're *my* girl, I think I can do this myself."

And he did.

No wonder the English and the Irish have been fighting all these years. The Irish'll drive you crazy. But you'll love every minute of it.

But *my girl* was destined to become *my wife* in the dim future. I had one more test. The temper test. I had to know before I became any more involved in this relationship.

After all, he had risked rejection by dating _____. I had to be willing to risk rejection by deliberately making him mad.

It wasn't easy for me. It's not my nature to go around trying to make people mad, especially anyone I was beginning to fall head over heels in love with. But I wanted to be loved in return. That picture of his mom haunted me. I had to know. *Was it me she objected to? How could it be? She had just met me. Would it be any girl he brought home? He just took me by My home was always open to guys. I guess sons don't take girls home.* I knew so little. I needed to know so much. Especially about temper. My papa had one, but he knew how to control it.

Since I was brought up in a hotel, being pleasant was a must. I was never allowed to show my temper, was encouraged to walk it off, work it off, or go to my room until I cooled it off. Not unleash it on unsuspecting, innocent people. We were of English heritage. We fought with cold, calculated words. Emotional outbursts belong to the uneducated, the uncouth.

English fury is the worst kind. If King George III were alive today, I wonder if he'd want us back? My father was French Huguenot—emotional, expressive. Where else but in France can you complain to your wife that your girl friend doesn't understand you? No wonder I'm so crazy, mixed up. Part of me says, "Do it," and the other part says, "Don't you dare."

It is no problem knowing when Chief's displeased. He doesn't hide it, but it took a run of these exercises before I suffered through the "very expressive" blatant period. Wow! Bingo! I hit the jackpot. He blew up and made no bones about it. It was so horrible, so bad, I was quaking. I cringed. I can't stand loud voices anyway. Big, booming voices I run from. Thank God, we were alone. He looked like a madman with eyes blazing. Words flew out so fast, so loud, it hurt my ears. Listening was impossible. I felt nauseous. Sick. What a fool thing I did. I wanted out. I always went "out" when I get in those situations. We were riding in a car.

"Out. Out." I looked up. I was in front of my house. I opened the door. He drove off so fast, I can still hear those squealing tires. I fled upstairs to my room.

"Libbylove? You okay?" Mom came to my bed. "Those tires could wake up the dead."

"I wish I were," I moaned.

"Can't be that bad." She patted me. "Temper test? That's it. Right?"

"Oh, Mom, I'll never see him again," I grabbed her. "It was horrible, just horrible."

"You just had to know it."

"What a fool I am."

"You had to know it," she rocked me. "Everybody has a boiling point. You wouldn't want a guy with no temper."

"I wouldn't?" I sat up.

"No. Used in the right way, it's a real plus. That's drive. It just has to be channeled."

"I'll never see him again," I wailed.

"When he cools down, he'll realize that's *not* your normal behavior, that you don't go around trying to make people mad. You wanted a temper test. You got it."

Rest assured, I never went around trying to make Chief mad. I have unknowingly, innocently, but never deliberately. Not me, I'm chicken. I'd rather love than fight. Disagreeing is different. Anyone who claims they've never had any disagreements will lie about other things, too. Right?

They keep telling us marriages are made in heaven. So are thunder and lightning. Through the thunder and lightning of my marriage I've tried to act as a lightning rod. I've been everything from a mediator and interpreter to a doll you stick pins in. But never a doormat. Sometimes I thought I was being angelic, when I was probably angling. I haven't seen any angels hovering over our neighborhood or in Bedlam. But I have tried to be cooperative—someone Chief could have a wonderful evening with.

As they say, the dear Lord must have loved the common people, he made so many of us. We are fascinating humans. The human I tried to study was my man. I've tried to analyze, not criticize; please, not displease; help, not hinder; face, head on, any difficulties (not tiptoe around). That includes temper. I refuse to fight fire with fire and add to the fuel. I've learned it blows over much faster. Besides, when you love someone, you want them to be happy. Chief was blessed with a happy disposition. I didn't want to change it.

Let's never forget: you cannot change another person. If you've tried, don't. Persuade, yes. And example is the best way. You'll only antagonize or lose them if you do otherwise. That's playing God. Maybe God wanted them the way they are since He made them. How do we know?

Only God can change a person. If we take care of that log in our own eye, we'll be busy enough (see Matt. 7:3).

That goes for temper pots also. Why not study, learn, and analyze what makes them sad? What makes them glad? What makes them mad? The first giant step is when we admit that everyone has some temper. Everyone not only has a temper, we all have a defect, a weakness.

My weakness is the worst kind. I get mad about once every five years. Very few things and very few people have the ability to make me really mad. Only people, things, and events I'm very emotionally involved with can have this power. Then, worse still, it's cumulative. When that last straw breaks or if someone steps over that line I try to draw very close around me, watch out.

Then I am totally out of it. I don't know what I do, but this I know: everybody laughs. The more they laugh, the more irrational I become. My defense is flight. How's that for the brave and the free to act? If humanly possible, I leave the scene. I usually walk or run as fast as I can. I wouldn't dream of driving. It's too dangerous. The times I have, I drove out of sight.

When I do come to, I try to figure out where I am and how I got there. Then I stop and think. Sort out my thoughts. My emotions. I'm drained. When in a situation—like with nine kids—where I can't leave, I find some quiet spot. Then I go into an exercise routine. If someone saw me, I'd die. For mild irritations, I used to play the piano. It doesn't work with kids around. It irritates them.

When I think I'm under control, I return either physically and/or emotionally. I always speak to people around me, even to the one straw that broke the camel's back. To me the cruelest form of behavior is the silent treatment. It's the deadliest. I don't mean you have to be Chatty Cathy. I do mean you owe it to another human being to at least acknowledge their existence.

Love means saying we are sorry. From a Christian standpoint, love is not possible unless there is the opportunity to say, "I'm sorry. Please forgive me." If Jesus truly came into the world to save sinners as the Bible teaches, we may conclude they are not only sinners but that those sinners must own up to their faults and confess they are sorry. If there were no sin in the world, there'd be no need for forgiveness, much less redemption.

We need to be forgiven. We need to forgive. How affecting and loving forgiveness can be! Warm and penetrating. We'd feel lost without it. Our Heavenly Father loves and forgives us. We are undeserving and wasteful of our gifts, but He doesn't wait for us to come groveling. He meets us with a welcoming embrace, not the silent treatment or a burst of anger, even when He has every right to be mad at us. From my combings, I learned some interesting things about temper.

Anger is a chosen emotion. Imagine that. It is an urge to attack when it doesn't get its way. No one can be made angry against his will. (That's why it took me so long to get Chief angry the first time, I suppose. I'm no psychologist. A paper psychologist maybe. A graduate of the School of Hard Knocks, for sure.)

When your desire is unfulfilled, you didn't get your way, it's wondering time. Wonder what desires could provoke someone to such anger? Experts in the subject tell us four reasons could provoke anger: power, self-sufficiency, importance, perfection.

If anger isn't an automatic reflex, what is it? I thought it just erupted, involuntarily, after provocation. You've seen it. The least little thing from an unwanted red stoplight to a ringing telephone will bring an explosion. Seems too mild for it to evoke such strong reactions.

In fact, they say some marriages should be told in a scrapbook.

If you were able to ask an angry person why he's angry, or what would he feel if he weren't angry, he'd say, "Peaceful, calm," accompanied by a "Think-I'm-stupid?" look.

This is what they say, but according to psychologists, when the angry are encouraged to pursue their true feelings, they discover this isn't true. They're only fooling themselves. Nobody else. The greatest con job we do is on ourselves. Experts claim that, most of the time, unrealistic expectations cause anger. Certainly to expect the stoplight to be green everytime you run through it is not only unrealistic, it's silly.

Angry folks choose to act like this to prevent a loss of self-esteem. It provides a buffer against humiliation. Low self-esteemers need their anger to support their fantasy that they're indeed as powerful, self-sufficient, important, and perfect as they wish they were.

As if this little info about anger weren't enough to set you thinking, then the realization hits you. Actually their anger keeps them from the feeling they profess to desire. Peace and tranquillity. Anger not only gives them intolerable emotions and depression, but worse yet a loss of their much desired good-guy image, their image of competence, or their illusion of greatness—traits they long for.

They want a good-guy front so much, they'll go to great lengths to deny, cover up, and control this darker side of their personality. They know short fuses really beget greatness. Or give a competent, "good-guy" image.

Try as hard as they may, in spite of their verbal attempts to keep in control, their body language gives them away. A dead giveaway is their demeanor. Even attempting to look pleasant, there's the telltale frown with tightly drawn lips, cold eyes, crossed legs, and folded arms across the chest. Experts say you can see it in their tapping fingers, bouncing feet, pushing thumb and fingers together. Sitting straight forward in their chair.

So study your mate for these symptoms unless you like living dangerously. Remember, marriage is an adventure. It can be a dangerous one, a fun one, an interesting one. It's all in how you look at it.

We'd be pretty stupid not to notice the red flag signaling "danger ahead." Can you tell when it's going up? Some swear, spit, or argue. Some walk away. Others give others the silent treatment. As the famous line goes—"I don't have ulcers. I give them."

When I began to realize that anger largely results from unrealistic expectations, that signalled my stop and think. What are some realistic expectations for me? For Chief. For my children? My friends? Like everything else, they're ever changing. As we all are ever changing.

Stop, look, listen, and think. People (including ourselves) who do possess more realistic expectations about themselves (and other people) seem to experience much less anger.

Have you noticed that, even though marriages may be made in heaven, the details have to be worked out down here? This fear of rejection is deeply buried, they say, in all of us. Some are more thin skinned.

During the early stages of relationships, this rejection, this sensitivity, can be especially acute. The younger we are in a relationship, the experts claim, the more tendency we have to try to show ourselves in the most favorable light. Understandably so. Everyone understands that honey attracts. Not vinegar. A clever woman is one who knows how to give a man *her own way*. Then you have the shy, demure type. Only look for one thing in a man—a rich father.

Sometimes we try to guess what another wants or likes. Especially the silent type. The non-expressives. Some women really go for the silent type. They think they're listening. Trouble is, when we think we know what images they have of us, then we have a tendency to try to adjust our actions and ways to accommodate, to fulfill that image. Sounds just like the perfect wife, doesn't it?

Worse still, we might unknowingly create an image we can't live up to, for images do create expectations. Before we know it, we're trapped, caught in our own web that we've woven in order to avoid rejection.

Caught in this web of pretense, if we realize we created it, that reveals our real feelings and preferences. We have every right to fear we might be rejected. That's why there's nothing so risktaking, so adventuresome as marriage.

If our marriage has any real solidity that our Lord taught us, there's little danger the rejections we encounter will be anything more than molehills. So don't make mountains out of them. A partial rejection means the rejection of only one idea. You can't win 'em all.

Because you can't have your way all the time doesn't mean you're being totally rejected personally. It's a two-way street in marriage. Sometimes we feel the need to reject the wishes of our mate. And rightly so, sometimes by actions, sometimes verbally.

"How can you talk to me like that," I wailed, "after I've given you the best years of my life?"

"Yeah?" Chief retorted, "And who made them the best years of your life?"

As usual, he's so right.

Anger is one of the main causes of the breakdown of marital communication. We already know why we get angry. Face it. Anger is a vital, valid natural emotion. It's neither right nor wrong, just part of the human condition. What is important is the way it's released and exercised.

If you're the temperpot, remember: anger, like any other God-given trait, has its positive side. It can be a survival technique. (See Amos 5:24.) To see people hurt, taken advantage of, suffering needlessly makes us angry. This righteous indignation often propels us to straighten out wrongs.

Sometimes we can get mad for no noble reason. That's because we can't have our way. Those who, consciously or unconsciously, have everyone do *what* they want, *when* they want, really strain to the hilt the relationship with their spouse. (See Jer. 12:9.)

We know plenty of words to describe angry people. The Bible abounds with them. It tells us the cloaks anger wears and hides behind. Read Ephesians, Mark, Proverbs for starters. Ephesians and Colossians caution us not to ever let our wrath last until the sun goes down. Proverbs tells us to express anger by redirecting it.

Repressed anger. Not accepting the fact we're angry is a common Christian practice. Some are taught it's a sin. Therefore, anger's unacceptable. Untrue. Anger is God given—an emotion that is a vital part of our personality.

Repressed anger is like a time bomb, a famous psychiatrist said.

Most normal folks don't want to be out of control. I know I am not proud of my anger. I feel better if I can confess I'm mad. I'm trying to put a stop sign out. Not a bad idea. But I have to be oh, so careful to say it in a tone of voice my beloved can accept.

"Honey, let me take a deep breath and start over. I think I'm beginning to lose my cool."

Experts say, never, but never, say, "You make me *so* mad." Immediately the defensive armor of your mate runs right up into place. They never hear another word spoken. It intimates they're to blame. We mustn't forget our original lesson: we chose to be mad. We're responsible for our own emotional reaction towards our mate.

Better still, try to say, "I'm sorry I'm angry. I surely want to work this thing out. Any ideas?"

To admit we're angry at least gets it out in the open. Of course, to admit anything is difficult for some. By the time we're able to admit it, we're displeased. And it's pretty obvious. Remember the body language?

Try to get control of your anger before it controls you. I'm a fine one to talk. I've already told you how out of control I can get. But I'm making progress. Now that I've learned I have a choice, I try not to let those little things pile up that set me off.

I realize God's not through with me yet. (see Eph. 3:16-21.) I know that conflict and disagreements are part of life. Isn't it a shame the word "conflict" strikes such terror in our hearts? We think of war and cruelty. Sure it means a fight or battle. But it also means a clasp or sharp disagreement of interests or ideas.

There is nothing fatal about that.

"It takes two to tango." It takes two to argue. Each is prone to exaggerate. It can be quite personal, loaded with false pride. Condescending. Unfair. As all the uglies surface, both mates really feel bad. Ashamed. But there are rules. I stumbled across some goodies:

1. Stop. Be quiet. Listen. Speak only when your spouse asks you to.
2. Suggest some rules agreeable to both. (I always say, if I know the rules, I can play the game.)
3. Try to bring out all the things, points, bones of contention you couldn't face while arguing.
4. Try your level best to be impersonal, objective.
5. Set a time limit for each to respond to the other's view.
6. No interruptions allowed, but if there's anything left to argue about, don't. Separate for an hour. Think and pray alone.
7. Write down all your spouse's points. Consider them. Mull over 'em. Be as honest as you can.

I've found I usually win by yielding. Yielding is different from losing. Think. Quarrelsome people squabble at nothing. Yak. Yak. That's exactly what they win. Nothing. If you listed your win-lose records like our favorite ball team, wouldn't it be dumb? Fruitless. Just shallow victories.

I drew my line long ago. Some things aren't worth bothering about: most criticism; accidental mistakes—mine and yours; results from others' ignorance or inefficiency; neurotic, paranoid ways people act; unsolicited advice or obligation; unavoidable, accidental losses in life; my imperfections as well as others'.

None of these things are worth arguing about. Would that bring change? Not worth losing good sleep, a friend, or mate over.

Laughing is much better than hitting. Learn to laugh. Cultivate that sense of humor. That's my broken record.

When you've tried every method you've heard and read about, and humor gets you nowhere, what else is possible to cope with an impossible person? Action. I call it the shock treatment.

Here is a five-step plan one family tried. It worked. This is one of my favorite cullings:

This particular pain-to-live-with would make Scrooge look like Santa. He was stingy. A pennypincher. Parsimonious. Simon Legree. Miser. Foams at the mouth even about utility bills. On top of that he is a martinet. A strict disciplinarian who makes life intolerable for people he lives with. Got the picture?

Five-Step Plan for Curing a Martinet

Be sure you have complete cooperation of the whole family.
1.   Secure permission of the family. Everyone has to participate.
2.   Tell absolutely no one outside the family your plan.
3.   Put the plan into action as dramatically and firmly as possible.
4.   Make it such a shock, such an explosion, so striking, the Raging Bull would not dare tell anyone or disown any of the children.
5.   When the crisis point arrives, give him an ultimatum. Stand firm. Stay with it.

Pick a day agreed upon. Disconnect lights, telephone and furnace or air-conditioner, according to the weather. Put all little appliances in the closet. Somehow, even put the toilets out of order in your bathrooms.

Serve dinner as it would have been before husbands had any modern conveniences. Dinner by candlelight. Warmed by fireplace. The more dramatic situation you can concoct the better. One that shows his inconsistencies. That shows the family is going to give up modern ways that don't jibe with his very unreasonable, antiquated ones.

How did the plan work? Temperpot came home in his usual bad mood, ready to rake his family over the coals. The house was dark and cold. He snapped the light switch. Nothing happened. He walked around the house trying to get something going.

Then he saw his family lined up watching him. His wife and three teenage kids. He was too astonished, shocked, bewildered. In a word, undone.

First, they all lit into him at once. They told him they were through. Then one at a time they threatened to tell everyone how he behaved at home. He treated them like slaves. His wife was last. She said she'd leave him if he didn't change his ways from that night on.

The girls said they'd testify in court. The son capped it by reminding his dad the effect it would have on the business. That was the straw that broke the camel's back. They made him sign each of the four agreements. He signed, then promised them as reasonable of an independence as they could expect. He vowed to be more loving, kind, considerate.

Learn to treat debates, discussions, and differences of opinion as play. Be tolerant and of good humor. The moment someone becomes too personal, impatient, critical, judgmental, gossipy, or negative, leave the room. There's nothing in The Book that says you've got to stay around for that behavior.

If acceptance is all we'll settle for, we're in for a rough marital ride. This means neither of us in this marriage will be able to receive clear, valid info from the other. We'll never know if we've hit home or have any real impact. Neither will we know where we stand or what our mate feels, much less know when we're stepping over that live wire or they're stepping over the line we've drawn.

Be as honest as you can be.

All deep marital relationships must be based on absolute openness. It's not easy to take these risks of being rejected. But if we don't, they'll do us in later and make Mount Vesuvius look like a firecracker.

Oh, it might seem bewildering. Complex. That's the fun of it all. The adventure. Like carefully, prayerfully assembling a Christmas toy. No sting for sting. No heavies here. No good guys versus bad guys. No contest. It's teamwork, partnership, a joint effort. A divine creation called marriage.

It's fragile at first, but hang on. That beauty is still there. It will be more apparent as the years go on. More breathtaking.

Just be sure *you* contribute more mirth than misery.

God, Chief, and I are partners—joined together. Our good-hope ship can be tossed, turned, gotten off course. Even wander from its moorings. But after all these years, we know anger's not going to cause us to be beached or wrecked. Neither will we have to bail out. We'll cling together like dust balls.

Marriages may be made in heaven, but a lot of the details have to be worked out here on earth, especially how we deal with our tempers. That is what this book is all about. Anger provides plenty of misery. We are like steel. When we lose our temper, we are worthless.

6

Fanning the Flame or Stoking the Furnace? What You "Snow," You Reap

As the late actress Mae West quipped, "Marriage is a great institution, but who wants to live in an institution?"

If you feel like you're living in an institution, locked up in an impossible situation, it's time to stop and think. Do a marital checkup. We have physical checkups. We even have our tires checked. But a marital checkup? Are you kidding?

What you "snow," you reap. That's a fact, Honey. We could use a little flattery in our lives. A flatterer is someone you can appreciate—someone who convinces you that you are not alone in the way you feel about yourself. They put a little sparkle in your life.

Remember: dull, uninteresting things happen to dull, uninteresting people. You've heard it before and you will again. We learn by repetition.

So check yourself first. Am I fun to be with? Would I like *me* for a friend? Would I like to be married to me?

Give yourself an annual fun checkup. Just as important as your annual physical.

Marriage is a living, growing, alive, ever-changing condition. It needs regular tending to, like our bodies. You don't expect the physician to make you well. Heal thyself. You can't expect another person, even if you do warm their cold feet or bring them coffee in bed, to make you happy. As Abe Lincoln put it, "We'll be as happy as we make up our minds to be."

Marriage is never dull, just the participants. Marriage is an adventure like none other made up of moments of mirth, moments of misery. A friend at church one Sunday—one of my kneebuddies, we pray together

—said she couldn't understand how marriage could one minute be so wretched, and another minute be so wonderful. That's the mystery.

Since Adam and Eve we've been thinking about it. Other civilizations haven't taught us much about marriage, not the Greeks or Romans, the ancient Chinese or Japanese, surely not cultures like the Middle Ages. Knights in shining armor didn't do much better. The Renaissance societies of Europe didn't know the secret of a happy marriage.

Did they look happily married? Not that I could tell. Forget the pilgrims. What kind of a married life do you imagine the pioneers had traipsing across America? They took the Bible with them everywhere they went. You'd think they found some good hints in 1 Peter 3:7.

We've come a long way, baby, but in the wrong direction. Our moments of mirth and months of misery usually are of our own making. We all grow and develop in unpredictable ways. Yesterday's perfect match we gave thanks for somehow ended up being a miserable mismatch. Today's seemingly miserable mismatch in the next decade turns out to be ideal, brimming over with mirth and fun as well as love and fidelity.

Like one's own life, one's marriage goes through stages.

The first stage is usually a highly euphoric state. A love relationship often thought too hot to cool down. Neither partner can survive this high-intensity stage forever.

Some marriages you've seen couldn't cope with loss of any passion. You know the type. They're in love with love, not each other. When they can't sustain this superglow passionate state, they go to pieces. They feel there's nothing left to build on. Then it's downhill all the way.

I've seen it happen to seemingly intelligent people, especially men, mainly because many of them think they know all there is to know about love and romance. They think because they've snared one filly into a dark corner, they're experienced. Little do they know that experience is the stuff that, when you finally get enough of it, you're too old to qualify for the job. And wives, stay out of dark corners, unless you're there with your mate. A dark corner is a place where men get bright ideas.

One of the mysteries of marriage I've noticed is: Why do folks who willingly read, study, learn, and practice the skills necessary to bring desired results in their business careers or sports—are willing to take lessons, be coached, have mentors, in every facet of their lives, yet wouldn't dare be seen at the marriage counselor's or go off for a weekend with their mate for a marriage enrichment seminar. Why?

Once the female okays her man, she respects him. Convinced he has the qualities to be father to her children, she can be more passionate, emotional, and romantic than any man ever was. Sometimes it's more than her mate bargained for.

In spite of doomsday statistics, most couples do survive the honeymoon stage. They actually enjoy settling down. It sounds so staid to some, even a trifle dull to others, especially their unmarried friends. It's anything but; it's quite an adventure, a balancing of mirth and misery, work and play. It is not wild passion becoming ho-hum affection. We're talking love—real love. That, too, is a balancing act.

At times you can *love* your mate more than you *like* him. Then other times you can *like* him more than you *love* him. Sometimes roles change. Sometimes you are the lover. They're the beloved. Sometimes you're the beloved, and they're the lover. Sometimes they fan your flame. Sometimes you fan theirs. It has to be one or the other, or nothing's going on. Maybe the fire's just banked, waiting to be rekindled.

The trait that strikes the death knell of marriage is *boredom.*

I can just hear their cries, "Why me? Why can't *he* be the one? Why is it always the female that has to keep a marriage interesting?"

The Dear Lord made females the responders. She is considered the homemaker, the Rock of Gibraltar, the brick. She realizes how very much the success or failure of the marriage depends on her. Females were created with special qualities—more sensitive, adaptable, flexible, equipped to be intuitive, prophetic, have the ability to "feel" what to do with personal problems, sensing the needs of others.

Most males, the experts tell us, throw all their energies toward furthering their careers, always coping with increasing competition, outside pressures. Home to them is and should be a haven, a rejuvenating, affirming place where a man can renew his energy and be accepted as he is—tired and worn out, often running scared.

Some Southern girls have a pipeline of advice handed down to them from their mom and grandmoms on how to treat a man. They like being a woman, are contentedly complimented to be called a "lady." They know not to nag, wheedle, whine, and worry a man to death. They don't compete with a man. They cooperate. They try to learn what makes him happy. No matter what kind of day she's had, he's number one at night.

I trained my troops never to ask, worry, or even speak with Chief until he had relaxed, taken his shoes off, and put his feet up. We took him the evening paper and gave him a refreshing cold drink. When he was ready to talk, he would. We did everything possible to make him happy, even if it was leaving him alone.

In public, you're careful to laugh at all his jokes even if you've heard them thousands of times, even if it's one you told him. You listen to his sports stories, accompany him to games, church, civic, social events. Never disagree with his views in public. Uphold his public image. Defer decisions to him. Declare him Numero Uno, even if he or the children know better.

It's a trade-off. If you uphold his public image and take care of his basic needs. Then you are free to do your thing with his blessing and support. This is not degrading compromise; it's a trade-off.

Trade-offs are made every day in our public and private lives. They mean, "you be good to me and I'll be good to you." A trade-off employs intuition, empathy, and kindness, not to mention self-confidence, poise, and good common sense. Christian value systems and styles of behavior are never static—the same year after year. Good taste and a touch of class survive. Not stuffy, square, out of touch with today's pace of instant everything.

Most things take time to mature, improve with age. Marriage is certainly one of them. It gets better with time. With plenty of generosity, compassion, and dedication, it can contain and deliver more mirth than misery.

The man's public image is enhanced by the beautiful woman he escorts. Make sure you're as good-looking as possible with what God gave you. Why? Because beauty is number one with men, according to today's psychologists.

None of my observations, how-tos, or hints are totally original. They are a compilation of all I've been told by my mom and other peoples' experiences, reading, observation, learning about the most fascinating of all of God's creations—men!

I was blessed to have grown up surrounded by men. My father's hotel was in a college town when the student body was 99 percent male. Besides my father and two older brothers, I had scads of male cousins. These observations include Chief, the star of our family, and seven sons, two sons-in-law, and ten grandsons. Obviously, I know more about what attracts men than about the birds and the bees.

Men want to date and marry a beautiful woman. Luckily, beauty is in the eye of the beholder. Everyone has his preferences—fat, skinny, blonde, brunette, redhead, short, tall. They have their list of most-admired parts of a female.

Men flirt and kid more. Naturally, a woman who is the recipient of this behavior—treated and greeted warmly—flirtatiously reacts the same way. Females of my generation appreciated a wolf whistle. To me, wolf whistles are like train whistles. I love to hear them, even if I'm not going anywhere.

This same male who balks at even reading anything that might make his marriage or sex life better, the experts say, is the one who hits the depths if a split is inevitable. He's the one that's deeply depressed, extremely lonely, sometimes suicidal.

Whatever they imagined caused this split is all in their heads. The number-one reason is mostly lack of communication skills, leading to bottled-up feelings. Men fall in love faster and are just as vulnerable to the loss of love as they were susceptible. Many a man falls in love with a bust size and ends up with the whole girl. Usually the girl's looks are the main attraction.

Females, they say, fall in love at a much slower pace. They're more concerned with money. (Remember this is only one psychologist's opinion—female at that. Maybe it's because I was post depression kid with no money. Money wasn't a factor when Chief and I were courting. The psychologist did say it was not greedy materialism but a realistic evaluation. She could be right.) Money never made my hormones do jumpups.

With most men, life revolves around their work. Always has. Probably always will. A woman's life also revolves around *his* work whether she likes it or not, just because he's her man. Her world is her husband. A woman's decision to marry affects not only the rest of her life, but the lives of her children she hopes to bear. Knowing the difference between love and infatuation, she is slower to love. Hers is built on trust. Only when she thinks she can depend on this man—his honesty, integrity—does she dare take the risk. After all, she has the most to lose. It's still a man's world and she could be at his mercy.

Once the male has won her love, he gets the whole ball of wax. No holds barred. Sometimes it's more than he bargains for. H.L. Mencken (1880-1956), American editor and satirist, said it best. A classic:

> Marriage is a bargain, in which a man seldom wants ALL that taking a wife offers or implies.
>
> He wants at most, no more than certain parts. For instance—he may want a housekeeper to protect his possessions and entertain his friends. But may shrink from the thought of sharing his bathtub, shower or bathroom for that matter with anyone; Home cooking may be downright poisonous to him; He may yearn for a son to carry his family name—yet suffer acutely at the mere approach of relatives-in-law; He may dream of a beautiful, warm, loving bedroom playmate and stand aghast at admitting her to his bankbook, his family tree and his secret ambitions; He may want company and not intimacy, or intimacy and not company; He may want a cook and not a partner in his business, or a partner in his business but not a cook. But, in order to get the precise thing or things he wants, he has to take a whole lot of other things that he doesn't want—that no sane mind could imaginably want.

Men will tell you it's your pleasing personality, nifty hobbies, sparkling conversation, your self-confidence, your affectionate nature, independent spirit. But the truth is, your beauty is number one—probably more important to his sense of prestige than sex appeal. Whatever it is that evokes his fantasy.

A leading female psychologist declares that men think beautiful women are better bedfellows than a plain woman. Yet they'll declare she'd be "the best mother of my children, most honest, good friend, most feminine." Forget it. If you don't think there's a difference in what a man *says* and *thinks,* you're not very observant of men. You'll see for yourself, if you're a manwatcher, professional eavesdropper like myself.

To abandon the project of trying to make yourself as beautiful as possible—to not make the effort—is not only dumb, it could be downright tragic.

So you're no Raquel Welch or Brooke Shields. Whatever your man's ideal is, don't let that discourage you. (Raquel and Brooke didn't look like that when they were born.) Work on your beauty, but most especially your inner beauty.

Negative thoughts, the narrowing of eyes, the furrowed brow, the thin, tightly drawn lips, spoil all chances of being beautiful. Suspicious women are homely. Jealousy, possessiveness, and resentment are all traits that drain the warmth from their expressions. A woman's greatest beauty potion is her own sweetness. By keeping her own expression clear, receptive, open, and fresh is better than any wrinkle-free cream. There's nothing prettier than a female filled with God's love and Holy Spirit.

You can acquire verbal, cerebral, libidinal dazzle. It's worth the time and money. Those minutes you spend in front of your makeup mirror are not vanity on your part. My mom said it's being considerate of those who have to look at us. It's good manners.

Chief calls females who don't wear makeup "unpainted barns." He says, "Who looks at them?" Some folks make fun of those who attempt to make the most of their looks. Consider it competitive, manipulative. Others think health, exercising, good grooming are unimportant or downright boring.

The way we move, stand, dress, and present our rosy, cleanly scrubbed face talks. It says we care, that we have the right kind of pride in ourselves. Therefore we are worth caring about. And we care about our husbands. It shows we think they're worth caring about.

My mom said, " 'Libbylove, always look your best, then forget it. Then you're free to think of others. You can relax because you're together. Then concern yourself with everything and everybody around you."

Don't be a bore, constantly griping, pulling, or adjusting something. Make sure you're together, well-glued, before you leave home. We should never apologize for our looks or talk about our beauty rituals in public. Men aren't the least bit interested.

If you're caught face-naked, it's not like being body-naked. You won't be stoned. Life goes on. You can survive. No mouthwash, toothbrush, or toothpaste? Borrow his. Suck a lemon or lime or rinse your mouth with salt water. That's good for your gums as well as your breath. There's no excuse for bad breath. Keep kissable.

A man wants to be around someone he's comfortable with. Tie a scarf around your hair, rather than scream, "Don't mess up my hair." A dress too tight to move in or cuddle in is bad news regardless of the price.

A loved body looks it—well groomed, clean, and healthy. Love it and everyone else will, too. It's your gift from God. Cherish it. It's the only one you'll ever get. It doesn't have to look lumpy, lost, and unhappy. Talk to your body, so when it moves, it says, "I am woman. I love being me. I am lovable."

Some movie stars have as many as twenty-five makeup men assigned to do their face. But there's help for us, too. If beauty consultants are not available or out of your price range, study magazines. The pictures may be exaggerated to make a point, but you can usually glean some pearls from the pages.

It's amazing how attitudes have changed. Twenty years ago if you wanted to see women wearing pin curlers, you had to go to a beauty parlor. Now you just go to the supermarket on Saturday afternoon. Men detest them.

Chief has never seen me with my hair rolled up more than four times in the nearly five decades we've been married. No, I don't have naturally curly hair. I roll it up when he's not around. Chief asked me once if they named the curlers *pin* for the heads they go on! He never fails to remark when we see these women running all around everywhere, some without a scarf on, "Who do they want to look good for? What about those of us who have to see them?"

The first person he saw running around in public like that—he simply stopped and stared. Not only that, she had on an apron in the grocery. He hasn't quit talking about the way she looked. We were living in a tiny town in Georgia. He came home with the news, "Honey, I found out she just moved here from a town way up North." His face showed relief. "I *knew* she couldn't be from around here. If she's Mrs. Bill Bailey, no wonder he hasn't come home! I hope she's not starting a trend." She must have.

Chief's figured out women pin up their hair even if they're *not* going out Saturday night, so they'll *look* popular. To this day, where we live, it's a label that says, "I'm from someplace else."

We all have our pet peeves—our list of Tackies or Uptowns, Prouds or Sorrys—from chewing gum, blowing and smacking bubble gum, to getting into a car in the rear-up position. If you're guilty of biting your fingernails you make the Tacky List. If you talk about your bodily functions or ailments in public, you head the Tacky List.

When your spouse is in a sharing, caring mood, get him/her to tell you their pet peeves about your looks. If your mate doesn't even know the color of your eyes, much less gives his opinion about what looks good on you, just observe. Those stingy with compliments usually are generous with criticisms. So stop and think.

One of my best friends had a hubby who wouldn't allow her to wear eye makeup. But you had better believe he eyeballed the chicks who did wear it. There are places that not only sell makeup but teach you how to apply it.

Style is an individual thing. Keep in mind just because "they" are wearing something that you've no business wearing, don't, if it doesn't bring out your best points or cover up your worst. So many clothes designers are males of questionable gender who hate women. They're mama-bashers. They sit around and scheme. "How can I make her look ridiculous this year? She'll wear anything 'they' wear. How can I make her more uncomfortable? What shall we pinch this year?"

Believe me, if you wear some of these far-out clothes, the only place you'll get pinched is your pocketbook. You don't have to look like Giggles behind the counter. Who knows what she looks like out from behind all that merchandise? Naked midriffs or shorty shorts that catch your mate's eye doesn't mean he wants *you* to wear them, even if you'd look better in them than Giggles.

Remember we're talking about fanning the flame, not dousing it. Most marrieds don't need advice about that. A friend's husband was bemoaning the fact that the romance had gone out of his marriage. He declared the most he'd seen in the last six months was a passionate nudge. He remembers the times his bride used to complain, "Oh, Harry, you're interested in only one thing." Now he declares he can't even remember what it was.

Undressing is an art. Few females learn it. Too many just start peeling. Some step out of their puddle of clothes. Others toss them here and there, then start slopping around in floppy houseshoes and housecoats.

Me? With nine children, I've been known to finish dressing in the car—so little time for me, and I have been known to start undressing in the car en route home. So exhausted, I start peeling the minute I climb into the car. I can't wait to hit the sack. I do go to sleep as soon as my head hits the pillow. But I do wake up.

However, my line is, "If you're going to keep me awake, keep it interesting."

One of my stupid habits? I undress in the closet, if available. If not, I slip on my gown or robe, tent fashion. Then I start peeling underneath it. Clothes puddle around my feet. Why? Only thing I can figure is my hotel unpbringing. I always felt surrounded by people—strangers. This wasn't true. I had private quarters. My mom was a private person. I never saw my mom undressed. She never came out of her bedroom unless she was fully dressed, face on, smile on, in control.

My two daughters are almost as prudish. I wondered if they could give up their granny gowns and pajama bottoms they used to wear before they were married. They did. Like myself, they keep the lingerie manufacturers, as well as their hubbies, happy. Happy hubby is their goal.

Never could understand why a woman lucky enough to have a good husband wants to look her best for outsiders, instead of dressing like the "star" she should be in her own home.

Now I'm not as bad as one of my friends who even wears her makeup to bed. Her husband thinks it's her natural beauty. She removes it in the morning after he leaves for work and replaces it before he comes home. She declares that the dear Lord left out eyebrows when he constructed her. It's hard for me to believe, she is such an artist with a makeup brush.

I don't go to that extreme. But I'm not an "oily-to-bed-oily-to-rise" type either. I want to look good to Chief at all times. But not too good. I'm already in enough trouble.

Do these survival kits, tidbits, and helps to fan the flame only apply to the wife? Absolutely not. Just as boring, uninteresting things happen to boring, uninteresting people. According to psychologists, attractive people attract attractive people. Moderately attractive people attract moderately attractive people. Unattractive attract unattractive. Of course there are exceptions. They've found about 85 percent who dated were about even in looks.

So stop and think. Stop and look. How attractive are you?

Are you the type who gives an automatic handshake? No clutch? Not really dirty but looks anti-laundry? So awkward you're like a wrestler at a tea party? Subtle—like a sailor on a weekend pass?

Men can read, I've noticed. No reason why they can't read etiquette books. Check men's mags to see what alternatives to their polyester suits are available. I don't pick out Chief's clothes unless invited. I picked out a lovely suit I thought would look good on him, priced so reasonably. But being that post-depression kid, he said, "Reasonable? Just two installments and a change of address."

You don't have to be a fashion plate. But you could at least be clean. Just because you didn't jog, play tennis, or break a sweat doesn't mean you don't need to take a shower. You're really too old to remain a flower child. The way the flower children smelled, you could tell they were using a little too much fertilizer. After all, hippies marched to the beat of a far-off drummer. And if you've ever smelled one of them, you know why he was far off!

What about a male personality checkup?

There is only one perfect Man, and they crucified Him. The Good Book is full of good examples for males as well as females—Daniel and his good health habits, and Paul, who taught us so much about living with people, to name two.

So women run around in pin curlers offending those who have to look at them. What about men? When you're waiting for the light to turn green, steal a glance at the guy in the car in the next lane. What's he doing? Either picking his teeth or picking his nose. Then when he gets wherever he's going, he probably picks on people around him.

There are some things you wait and do when you have to go to the little-boys' room. Picking your teeth and picking your nose are the two more important ones.

Does the wife have to acquire all the charm in the family? Be the only one who has flawed character traits? You know the cold remedies that let you sleep for eight hours? He takes two of them. You used to think he couldn't get you on the sofa fast enough. Now he can't get you off fast enough, so he can nap. I don't know what he's saving himself for, or where he left his energy. But he never studied Ben Franklin. Ben said, "Sleep? You've got that *long* sleep coming." So don't cop out with sleep, or drop out of the action. You only have today. Live it. Thank God for it. Enjoy it. Make somebody else enjoy it. Who have *you* made happy today?

Shape up. Don't be so dumb you think charisma is a Mexican curse, so pessimistic the only thing you expect to get on a silver platter is tarnish. Don't be so shallow, if it weren't for bumper stickers, you wouldn't have any opinions at all.

I've seen a male "into religion," he claimed. But he's the kind of guy who would put in a slug to call Dial-A-Prayer. So self-centered, if he had been at the Last Supper, he's have worried about the calories. Cheap? If he had been at the Last Supper, he would have asked for separate checks.

That beauty, good looks stuff that males insist upon now should include their own. Divorce has put a lot of men back on the street. As the ancient expression goes, "A man in the house is worth two in the street." Rest assured they're the ones that look good, feel good, and smell good.

Male cosmetics and grooming aids are not only an integral part of the mating system, they are big business. Men are buying, trying. They've heard of the Pumpkin Eater who had a wife and couldn't keep her. Put her in that pumpkin shell where he kept her very well, probably because he didn't smell. Fear of divorce is influencing husbands to take more notice of their own looks, be more careful of their own grooming.

I can just hear you say all this is "so secular," of the world. As God's children, we certainly want to be God's beautiful people. Beautiful people are not the jet set. They're Spirit-filled, beautiful people inside out. They know this wonderful mechanism—our body, our gift from God—is His temple.

Have you ever wondered why so many beautiful women are married to men with a good case of ugly? Women understand. We know. We want *more* than good looks in a husband. Ambition, integrity, intelligence, and good humor rate way up on their list. Along with tenderness, sincerity, and a sense of responsibility, especially fiscal responsibility.

I enjoy the enthusiastic, alert, aware, alive, ready-to-go quality that Chief has in addition to the most important. He is a *good* man. Good is a beautiful word. God made the world and it was *good*. In my book, it hasn't changed. "A good man nowadays is mighty hard to find."

Chief's bubbly personality, quick wit, great sense of humor, and zest for life attracted me, kept me interested. His positive attitude, optimism, and ambition endeared him to me. His sense of responsibility was outstanding. A hard worker, who could give up the good time of the moment for a longtime goal, convinced me finally that he was husband material in spite of my reservations. His kindness and consideration for others and his ability to cry as well as laugh were bonuses.

No, being goodlooking doesn't hurt, if you're male. It might definitely attract you to the opposite sex and vice versa. But it won't keep a mate.

Sometimes your mate can be a priss or a primitive (smell like a goat)—according to how he was raised. Some males just don't like water, period, except to fish in. Reward is what it's all about, praise. I never could decide when I enjoyed loving my own little boys more—when they were asleep or after their bath. I always asked them for a hug. Their little clean bodies clinging to me for their goodnight hug was a ritual. I at least got a hug and kiss on the back of the neck from my teens. Nothing is more enjoyable than a clean body. You don't have to smell as sweet as sandalwood, but you don't have to smell like dirty socks either.

How do you get grown males to get the message, "Cleanliness is next to godliness"? And if you want to know the magic elixir, cleanliness is how you get next to me. I'm sure there are other wives who share my sentiments. How do you let your mate know without offending him? Your best bet is to give him a gift set of grooming aids. My little boys knew they'd get something that smelled good just like they knew they'd get something that read well, a book of their very own.

"This soap (or powder, whatever) smells so good. I think it would be great for you. I warn you, though, it'll make me want to be close to you." That's better than, "I love the way _____'s husband smells. He smelled just like _____. I think I got the brand name right."

Better still, invite your husband to shower with you. Soap each other. Share the good aroma and the fun. It's okay—you're married. Just start leaving the soap in the shower. A few snuggles would help.

First, last, and always, set the good example yourself. Check for other ways of saying, "I love you." Sniff his sneakers. Wash them for him. Start snitching his dirty clothes and washing them for him before he wears them again. Get together his travel survival kit. Pack things for his face, skin, and hair. Men are usually too busy to shop for themselves. Volunteer to help him select his clothes. He might be secure enough to let you into this male domain. It's another way to show you care. Men enjoy compliments as much as women do.

Attentiveness is the key. If you don't pay attention to him, somebody else will.

My special delight is cutting Chief's hair. It took me years to get up enough nerve to tell him I wanted to be his barber.

I discovered this joy when my own papa let me sit on his lap and comb his hair. It was almost a ritual, a rare pleasure, a bonding. He was always on the go, darting in and out of the hotel "tending to things." Nothing thrilled me more than the words, "Come on, Libbylove, I want you to comb my hair."

Papa would plop down in one of the big rockers lining the front porch of the hotel (1800s vintage). I'd crawl up on his lap. He'd hand me his little black comb that always stayed in his left pocket. I spent many happy times combing his hair. I thought that full head of white hair was the prettiest thing I ever saw. Set off his agate blue eyes. A hotel brat, I covered more laps than a napkin.

We rarely talked. He rocked back and forth gently, while I combed away. He smelled so good. Mom always said, "He's the bathingest man." The love between them was beautiful to see. Papa took great delight in pinching her when she passed by, giving me a wink. He'd chuckle at her reprimand. He loved to plant an unexpected kiss on the nape of her neck, lamenting, "Lula, that wisp of hair looks so lonesome." I thought she must have the most lonesome hair in the world. I thank God for stashing me into a loving home.

Visiting my college roommate and her husband one evening, she announced it was his haircut time. She whipped out her barber kit. He sat there like a lamb. I was so jealous. I watched, fascinated. He looked so happy, content, so loved. It gave me courage.

"Chief, I want to cut your hair." Chief succumbed. "Please let me try. You like short haircuts anyway. If I mess up, you've got enough length to get a barber to shape it up."

I've been cutting his hair for at least ten years now. It's one of the most pleasureable experiences I have. Maybe it's the nostalgic tie with my own papa. Chief keeps his comb and nail clippers in his righthand pocket. These are intimate moments etched in my memory bank—enjoyment, security, feeling loved. True in both instances, with Papa, with Chief. No words are necessary. Feelings of love, respect, thankfulness brim over. Here is the man who takes care of me in so many ways. He protects me, sees to it I have a roof over my head, am amply fed and clothed without a murmur of, "What's in it for me?" Like it's a delight, not another burden.

I can't and don't take these gifts from God for granted. It's okay to call me a leisure lizard. As I've said before, Chief makes the living, and I try to make the living worthwhile.

Being cared for doesn't mean a loss of my independence, self-determination of self-expression as so many women's libbers would lead you to believe. I'm well aware that dependency escalates. It can, if you allow it, go right on up to the point of no return where I could be at the mercy of the person on whom I'm leaning. No, I don't and won't turn my life over to anyone except my Heavenly Father.

Like every rational child of God, I want to be my own person, make my own decisions, take my own responsibility. I don't mind asking for

and accepting help when I need it. I think we all are uniquely rational
and irrational. I know that my distortions, crazy quirks, and ideas are
uniquely mine, just like my fingerprints.

So, each of us will have our own unique way to fan the flame, to keep
our marriages going and glowing. Full of more mirth than misery.

Right up there with your man's favorite meal, his undisturbed chair,
television, and books is sex. It might fluctuate in popularity, rating, or
frequency. Besides the birds and the bees, humans have participated in
this pasttime since Adam and Eve—even kings and queens, the guy next
door, the pastor in the pulpit.

The surprising thing? We know more about the birds and the bees,
kings and queens than we do about sex. There are enough delusions,
illusions, conclusions to go around, enough facts and fiction, adjustments
and maladjustments. To put it graphically, there's enough in print to
make you and me, too, go bananas.

We might do well to take our cues from chimps rather than shrinks.
They know all about "doing what comes naturally." They don't worry
about doing it right.

At best, giving oneself to your mate, willingly, uninhibitedly, is true
communion. We haven't been under a rock. We're well aware we could
perform this physical act outside the confines of marriage. But we also
know we could never have the stirring, heartwarming, peak experiences
with someone we do not love. That includes a mate. So, as the Good
Book tells us, do yourself a favor: love your wife (see Eph. 5:25). It's part
of God's plan to keep the male around the house and for the female to
keep the home fires burning.

In Adam and Eve's time, when they began to multiply, the man
provided the food for the mother of his child. He also protected them
from wild beasts and other predatory males. No way would a mother
leave her child to look for food. Only her man could protect her, forage
for food for them that God provided.

How did the woman keep the man around? Availability.

You can readily see that those who talk about sex and read about it
often don't have it. If availability is not taken advantage of, marriage can
become a problem.

Availability is at different levels of a man's priorities for most couples today. Most mates won't stray because their bedfellow offers them sardines instead of caviar, hamburger instead of steak. Some would stray anyway. Others need only a little encouragement and are very vulnerable, Christian or not.

Boredom is the culprit. Remember: dull, boring, uninteresting things happen to dull, boring, uninteresting people, in bed also.

A steady diet of any of these offerings would be injurious to your intimate life. Variety is not only the spice of life, it's variety that definitely spices up your love life. You don't have to hang by the chandelier. He might really prefer more quietude.

How we hunger after life in all its fullness, especially the fullness of love. Say *yes* to life and *amen* to love. Real love cannot be imitated. Our care and concern for our mate must be genuine, or our love has no meaning. There's no way you can learn to live without learning to love.

The mention of the word "virginity" evokes different feelings, responses, and behavior in each man. Why are you, the virgin (which I was, by choice), the Mount Everest, the Matterhorn to some males? Why must you be conquered, persuaded, enticed, lead astray to become one more conquest?

Not me. I knew from day one the most important word in a female's vocabulary was *no*.

Word travels among the boys. They soon get the message. So conform and persuade attempts are appreaciated, but not the way, only the skirmishes. So my personal declaration of sexual independence was: I will go to bed only with the man I marry. (So bug off.) Consequently, I still have a host of male friends who not only respect me and care for me. They still think I'm fun to be around and seek my company. You can't have too many friends.

Since my wise editors didn't go along with my advice, "Liz Taylor should write this book, not Liz Griffin," you'll have to take my word for what I say. Some females have had more hands on them than a doorknob. But not me. Consequently, with my limited solo experiences, that's all I have to offer: nearly fifty years of more mirth than misery—married to the same man.

Consequently, all I know about sex and not afraid to ask, I owe to Chief. Since I was a warm, loving, giving person, I made an apt pupil. Remember I met him when I was fifteen, married him when I was twenty-three, had my first child at twenty-six. Just think how many children I could have had!

Here are some of the mysteries I've delved into, learning about what comes naturally after the wedding ceremony. These are not stark truths, probably coverups. The fun is finding out for yourself.

From my cullings, readings, and learning from authors that claim to be experts: Sexual satisfaction doesn't have to become a problem. If sympathy, persistence, intelligence, and true love reign.

By all means, read, learn, digest, and practice. But tread lightly. You can't expect overnight success, especially if you apply their written instructions. Go by their directions as you would for adjusting your carburetor.

Just as each person is unique, each has a unique approach to sexual satisfaction. There's no one way. No matter-of-fact, calculated, practical way. You can't approach the matter as you would a better way to brush your teeth. There again, the fun is finding out for yourself.

There is nothing mysterious about sex appeal. Whatever it is comes in the door with you. Charm has always been an essential to happiness. No one will develop your charm and personality if you don't. As you learn to give of yourself and touch the hearts of others, you will achieve their response. Get their recognition. You have to go for it. Keep practicing.

There'll always be men who dare not be assertive, and women who shun their sex appeal. Some are told the pursuit of these traits is selfish, a power play, nonsense. Must we live with drab women or timid men in the name of "goodness"?

No. Life is for living, celebrating, a gift from God. So is sex. Sex used in the right way, within marriage, is one of the best things in life. When blended with genuine love from God, it is ecstasy. It's an art, a science. It can transform you, put a bounce in your step, feed your intelligence, and intoxicate your spirit. Thanks be to God!

7

Stretch Marks:
What Mid-life Crisis?
Yours or Mine?

"It's the male menopause!"

"The what?" I asked.

Our family doctor repeated, *"Male menopause."*

"You mean I can't even do that by myself? He's gonna' beat me to it?"

"What do you mean, Libbylove?"

"I haven't been through menopause yet!" I reminded him.

"Mid-life crisis. Middle-age crazies. Thought you'd understand it more clearly if I called it the male menopause."

"Can't be. It's a misnomer," I insisted.

"Call it what you like, Libbylove," my doctor friend smiled, "Maybe you'd accept a female's interpretation. Dr. Joyce Brothers calls it the Pivotal Decade."

Pivotal? That word sounded threatening.

"Yes. A man's behavior can be so rash, so foolish. It's a very crucial stage. Dr. Brothers says, 'The quality and character of the rest of a man's life are actually determined during this stage.' That's why it's called The Pivotal Decade."

"Decade? *Ten years?* Are you saying ten long years?" It felt more like a sentence.

"According to the individual. Their ability to cope. They usually revert to their worst childhood traits."

"Oh, no," I moaned. "I can see it dimly."

"What?"

"Chief's temper. His mom warned me. The first time I met her, she said, 'Don't know why you want to date him. He's got the worst temper!'

I almost laughed in her face. Chief was a charm bucket. Through the years I figured she really didn't want any of her children to marry. I'd heard there're mothers like that. She never seemed to really like her in-laws. Maybe I was wrong. But certainly I was no threat the day she met me. I was fifteen years old. Marriage was the last thing on my mind."

"You two were teenagers when you met?" Doc asked.

"Yeah. That very emotional period. As they say—easy glum, easy glow!" Getting serious again, I rushed on while I had an audience, words spilling all over the place. "I hadn't thought about Chief's mom's assessment of his disposition until lately. His temper *has* been going unchecked. They say a man is never in worse company than when he flies into a rage and is beside himself. Not only has he been beside himself, he's by himself, except for me. The troops, our children, flee. Even the maid left. Maybe it's my imagination. Chief is not himself. That is *not* my imagination."

"Even our out-of-town friends ask, 'What's the matter with Chief?' His office help notices, too. My answer has been, 'I don't know,' because I don't know. But when his patients, who love him dearly, asked, I felt it was time to ask you."

"Male menopause." Doc smiled patiently. "Got it, Libbylove?"

I nodded. "Can anything be done to help him? He doesn't want to act this way, I'm sure. What can I do?" Questions tumbling over one another. The final one, "What can *you* do to help him, Doc?"

"Nothing."

"Nothing?"

"He hasn't asked me for help."

I was silent.

"Who does Chief listen to, Libbylove?"

"No one."

"No one?"

"Ask him. He'd tell you the same. I've asked him many times through the years. He just grins and says, 'No one.' Must be true. Ask his own family. I have. All say, 'No one.'"

More silence.

"How can I survive? I'm his target. The doll he sticks pins into. Nothing I do pleases him. Absolutely nothing."

The words oozed out like a lanced boil.

"I've tried it all." I tried to stem the verbal flow, remembering Doc was one of Chief's friends and golfing partners. We both loved Chief.

I tried to manage a laugh with, "Think of my alternatives. Mother of nine? Chief says if I were thrown out on the open market I wouldn't have a chance. He bears his misfortunes like a man. He blames everything on me!"

I did bring a smile to Doc's face. He knew I was serious. I felt the painfulness of telling a friend things I did not want to.

"How much do I have to put up with? Two are married. Two are in college. Five are still at home."

"You have to put up with everything but physical abuse."

"Mental doesn't count?" I asked.

"No," Doc rose, dismissing me. "You're tough, Libbylove. A survivor."

A survivor? On the way home thoughts whirled through my mind. Some sane. Some wild. Like wet leaves on a windshield: *A guy who says he never made a mistake may have a wife that did. There's no fool like an old fool. You can't beat experience. Don't get out the pitypot. The dear Lord said, It came to pass. He didn't say it came to stay. It's just a stage. Hang in there.* All this self-talk was interspersed with, "Thank You, Heavenly Father, for the good years, for the funtimes. There has to be a reason. Maybe no excuse—but a real reason for Chief's bizarre behavior. The Pivotal Decade. Huh? For Chief? For me? Our marriage?"

Once home in the safety of Bedlam, not behind the wheel, I felt full of peace. A feeling I hadn't experienced in a long time. I gathered the troops around me. It was time for a family meeting, a powwow. I told them what Doc had told me. I explained to the older ones the real reason for Chief's behavior. I told the younger ones that Chief wasn't himself. They were well aware of this. I talked with them about my need to get away, to think, rest, pray, and regain my perspective.

The younger ones were eager to go with me, to leave Chief with his own world. The older ones had jobs. They knew to keep out of his way unless, by chance, he showed signs of wanting their company. They knew how to handle the situation. They were wise beyond their years. They, too, loved Chief, even though he was unlovable at the moment. They promised to cling to the good memories and look for the good things. They all knew to be quiet, stay out of the way. Pray.

The place I can really get in touch with myself is by the ocean. Once there, I feel relief. Remind myself of my many blessings. Even though a little rain has to fall in every life, I know the sun is under there somewhere. I remind myself that each new day brings me another chance.

We each have our own way of trying to solve our personal problems. Granted marriages are made in heaven, but the details have to be worked on here. First. I try to examine myself, see if I like what I see in the mirror. I try to meet the crisis squarely, objectively, head-on. I didn't say it is easy. But I try.

This takes practice like any other habit or skill. Otherwise it is compromise. To me, compromise, like evasion, is the very essence of defeat. Marriage is full of compromise, I realize. There is a limit. I had reached it. I had felt defeated long enough. I had been, unknowingly, depressed and unhappy. I was prayerfully quiet. I listened to my mind. I asked God to speak through my mind, to keep it clear, unmuddled, unconfused, objective.

As I waited, thoughts twirled around my mind. I knew I had to *feel* before I could think logically. Let my emotions flow. I had bottled them up too long, too often, being a wife and mother of nine. I was too much the peacemaker. Was it worth the price? Surely I had observed how fascinating fussy females seem to be to some men. That's just not my style. Here, alone, I could let my emotions flow. Passion is an energizer for me. I was exhausted.

What did I feel? Anger. It drowned my defeated attitude, my depression. I had no desire to quarrel, to accuse, only to analyze, calculate, and plan.

Who was I angry with? Chief. It all started so innocently. The bad moods. First, they disappeared almost as soon as they came. I thought maybe he had a bad day at the office. 'Tis said home is a place a lot of

men go to raise a fuss because something went wrong at the office. I
checked with his staff. Just a "usual" day.

Then I thought he'd had a bad day at the golf course. The moods got
blacker. Closer together. Nothing I did pleased him. If I fed the children
before he got home, he asked, "Why? I want to be with them. After all,
I am their father. We are family." Or he'd say, "Why can't you feed these
kids *before* I get home? Can't you realize I need some peace and quiet
after a day at the office?"

"Why don't you get out and play tennis and golf? You used to." Chief
would say. "You'll never have any friends staying home. You never get
any exercise." So off I'd go to these two sports I formerly enjoyed. But
then when I got home if there was any little thing not done . . . and there
were lots of little things and big things, sometimes, not done at Bedlam.
I'd hear, "If you'd stay home with the children and tend to your business,
quit that golf and tennis, you'd get things done."

In a no-win situation, I chose the latter. I stayed home. Besides, I
didn't want anyone to know the misery of my marriage. It had heretofore
been mostly mirth, by far. I kept my distance as Proverbs 22:24-25
caution, "Keep away from angry, short-tempered men, lest you learn to
be like them and endanger your soul (TLB)." I had to be in control, stay
in control, for the children's sake as well as mine.

Who else was I angry with? Me. Why? I had compromised myself.
Tried to change myself for all the wrong reasons. After all, he had
criticized everything about me: my mental; my physical; my sexual. He
had questioned my behavior, my motives. Why did I try to change
myself? To keep peace, to please Chief. "To have a happy home."

Whenever angry, I walk, walk, walk. I try to analyze. I checked the
events leading up to this encroaching Pivotal Decade. I had read about
the female symptoms: A woman dyes her hair, redecorates the bedroom,
loses weight, does all sorts of things.

I recalled a depressing article written by a male psychiatrist. He had
said not to blame myself, not to do all these above things, unless I wanted
to. Don't take his disinterest personally, and think you are a failure.
There comes a time in some men's lives when it doesn't make any
difference how you present it, he won't buy it. I remember the cold chill

I felt. Maybe he was talking about me and I didn't know it. I was unaware.

I went over Chief's symptoms. I remembered defending Chief's actions, defending him against criticism from family and friends, covering up, making excuses. I didn't fool anyone, least of all my children. After carefully explaining it was my choice (aside from my duty), I promised to take care of myself. For them. For me. I was satisfied I had given all I had to this marriage. I had no more to give. Only wait and pray, stop and think.

I threw away my mental rosary of hurts, misunderstandings, and resentments. I shifted my thoughts from the past. As my mom said, "That's history."

Walk. Walk. Plan. Plan. *So I've made mistakes,* I thought. *I can still change. I can't change Chief. Never consciously tried. After all, I have always said the only time you can change a man is when he's in diapers.*

I can't change the personal hell he must be going through. I can change my attitude towards it. I can accept the need of more endurance. More patience on my part.

If Chief ever needed understanding, it is now. I always tried to give him "space." Now, more than ever, he desires it. The least I can do is oblige. If I'm the problem, remove myself. Wait in the wings for my cue.

I was full of vows: to renew my efforts to put myself in order; to be myself; to live every day; to keep my attention on the present; to be alert, to cultivate my guiding hunch, my constant conversations with the Dear Lord, watching, acting, keeping the intuitive, the initiative to change alive—not compromising myself.

I vowed *not* to assume Chief, who had caused me such difficulty and hurts, was always willful or even had me in mind. Maybe he was lashing out, giving "help, help" signals. But you can't help anyone if they won't let you. My every attempt was rebuffed. Nothing worked: sympathy, empathy, sense of humor. Maybe the hurts were unintended. I truly felt sorry for Chief. He was helpless. Treat a sick mind like a sick body, with the same mercy. A man without self-control, so says Proverbs 25:28, is as "defenseless as a city with broken-down walls (TLB)."

I had the choice of letting it devastate me or be a learning experience.

It was not going to destroy me. Proverbs 26:2 said, "An undeserved curse has no effect. Its intended victim will no more be harmed by it than by a sparrow or swallow flitting through the sky (TLB)." My problem? To be sure I didn't deserve this curse. I realize it's a good thing we don't always get what we deserve.

In Psalm 27, David pleaded, "Tell me what to do, Lord, and make it plain because I am surrounded by waiting enemies (TLB)." I need the Lord to make it plain. You know I never could add or subtract, only multiply.

After all, marriage is an adventure. Male menopause was an adventure for me—big time.

8

Confessions of a Professional Eavesdropper: Stop, Look, and Listen

Middle Age in Marriage is definitely the time to stop, look, and listen. It's that time of life that provides the most material for jokesmiths. I needed all the mirth I could get to survive this destined, dastardly decade.

Middle age is when your back goes out more often than you do. Middle age is when a night on the town is followed by two on your back.

A good sense of humor is a necessity to get you through the menopausal years. It rates right behind your great faith, remembering, "This, too, shall pass." If your male is somewhere between forty and sixty, these catch phrases might apply to him, according to which psychologists you read: Male Menopause, Mid-life Crisis, Middle-age Crazies. It's that long period between I-don't-care and Medicare.

Those around my mom could not tell she was any different in looks or behavior during menopause. It can certainly be true of males. But middle-age worries have an unsettling effect on men. Somehow they fear aging more than females. I don't know why.

Middle-aged women in our youth-worshipping culture are the ones in a real predicament. More often than not, the female is singled out as the butt of jokes. They are often ignored, presumed invisible, nonessential, roleless, even an embarrassment sometime.

Some middle-aged men seem to think all they have to do is have a young chick hanging on his arm, then they're automatically young. The stages of the female go from the "ingenue, the sex object, to the grandmother, the sage."

Our middle years, when it's perfectly possible for a woman to be sagacious and sexual, seem to make us uncomfortable. I read some male writer's account of the aging female. He compared her to mice. He said you don't really see them or hear them. But when you do, and your eyes make contact with their tiny beady ones, they scurry back to cover. Hiding. Especially when a male looks at them. Why? They are such sexual beings they are ashamed of their feelings.

That's putting it pretty strongly, graphically. Another writer compared them to elephants. The female elephant after her reproductive years knows it. The male elephants with their tusks herd the female elephants off into a group away from the action. Here they spend the rest of their days, sent off to die.

I checked one joke book in my collection. It had fourteen jokes about woman's looks.

There were six jokes about a woman's age. Thirty were about a woman's appearance.

But when the jokes are about beautiful girls, they are different.

Most jokes about women were put-downs: thirty-one were about women's clothes; eight about driving; nine about their hair, and six about their weight. The nice thing about it is that we can joke about each other. All we need is equal time. Chief and I do this. And I write about him in a weekly column I do for our newspaper. Your spouse or loved ones are the only ones you can joke about, write about. After nearly five decades, we can be comfortable with humor. The best idea is to make yourself the butt of the jokes.

The fact that females lives intertwine with those of their men make them vulnerable to the problems arising from male menopause. Being the butt of jokes is only one manifestations. In their unhappiness, men search for someone to blame it on. It hasn't changed. As the song says, "we always hurt the one we love."

Therefore, like a certain car-rental company, wives have to try harder during this decade, try to keep our sense of humor and not take it personally. We try to realize that, for many men, middle age is a time of dissolving dreams. They, too, are in the sandwich generation—caught between facing the decline of health or death of their parents and realizing children are leaving the nest.

Some men are overwhelmed with guilty feelings of not spending enough time with their children, not teaching them, not getting close to them. All these things give a man food for thought, a sense of his own mortality, the realization that he's probably lived the majority of his years.

This is the time he begins to question things like life's meaning, his own self-worth, personal value to society, his family, and community.

Little do men know or stop to understand that their spouses are going through the same thing.

Every fact of a man's life seems under seige. Sometimes they react wildly to the insecurity they feel. They do the craziest things: insist on selling the house; give up their job; cash in their insurance; hop a slow boat to China; write the great American novel; join the Peace Corps. Some do these things. I knew a professor who took off in a boat to the islands and stayed there, leaving his wife and children behind. You hear it more and more. Some do leave home. Others just act so crabby their spouses wish they would.

What is the underlying thread? The common denominator? He thinks only of *himself!*

Most reactions to these middle-life crazies have ranged from chasing cars to chasing women. Sensing life's passing him by, he reaches out desperately. He considers it the age between adolescence and obsolescence. When it comes to girls, he says, "I'm at the awkward age. Fifty-two." He's reaching out desperately. There's great pressure to "go for it," to get all the gusto you can while there's still time.

Often his spouse would love to join him in his crazies. His change of pace. His chasing his star. The song that says to turn around and look at *me,* describes the feeling. She has her needs, but often she's not in his plans.

Females know menopause is inevitable. It's part of the aging process for them. It usually occurs around age fifty. It's of shorter duration—approximately three years compared to the male's decade.

Medical doctors finally came up with the term, "climacteric." It's been assigned to describe the male's mid-life period, a time when there's a sharp drop in the level of testosterone, the male hormone. Like with the female, this is usually around age fifty. The diminishing of this male hormone, according to the medics, can cause males to feel just like females feel at menopause: hot flashes, dizzy spells, apathetic, depressed, chronic fatigue and headaches.

It's just like a merry-go-round of cause and effect.

Anxiety may make the testosterone level fall even more sharply, anxiety over their sex lives, anxiety over their jobs, anxiety over aging, even anxiety about death. Name it. You hear it in their jokes: "Life begins at forty. So does arthritis;" and, "Youth is when zing goes the strings of your heart. Middle age is when jiggle goes the jelly of your belly."

The experts emphasize that *all* men do not experience this drop in testosterone. They've found some eighty-to-ninety-year-old males have a level comparable to a twenty-year old. But they are the exceptions. Some men experience a sharp drop in their hormonal level. Others normally experience a slow, diminishing condition.

Studies show there's no close relationship between level of testosterone and sexual interest as long as testosterone remains in the normal range. One internist stated, "Potency is not a function of how much hormone you're secreting as long as you have enough."

However, even the influence of diminishing sexual prowess can psych some mid-life men into the pits of sexual anxiety. The psychological can be far more damaging than the physical. Fear sets in, fear of getting older, of not being able to perform. Add to that job stress, disenchantment with marriage or life in general, and it can be more devastating than the physical damage. This factor can play havoc with sexual life.

What's a good wife to do during this dastardly decade?

If you're a risk taker, you can always try to fan the flames one more time. Don't waste your time envying couples who seem happy together. I got so I couldn't stand to look at "romantic" movies or see couples obviously in love, enjoying each other. Thou shalt not covet. Thou shalt not be filled with resentment. Knowing our spouses are super sensitive about their sex life during this destined decade we should: make it as easy for them as we can; show our vulnerability, especially if we're usually the beloved, not the lover; allow ourselves to be the lover. Be sure to take the pressure of "performance" off of him. Show him you two have nothing to prove. Chief and I certainly don't. I'm sure you and your spouse don't, not to yourselves or to each other. Making love is not a battle or some sort of theatrical production.

If he's in a playful mood, just let him know you're the one who's making time for love, that you always have time. As delicious as spontaneity is, don't underestimate planned-for-sex. Chief and I can vouch.

If there's one more way you've thought of to keep your lovemaking fresh and varied, try it. But this isn't the time for weirdo stuff—the shock treatment. It's time for a truth meeting. A mutual give and take.

If you're willing to take the risk, you might infuse a new spark, a new energy or innovation. Men, like ourselves, want change, are easily bored. Yet at this time they can be leery of change, especially those they didn't initiate. (He won't kiss his wife for ten years, but will go out and shoot a fellow who does.)

The more a couple makes love, the less they make war, and the less likely they are to wind up in a divorce court.

Don't be fooled by your sexual feelings. Try to learn the difference between love and infatuation. Don't be fooled by outside pressure or the emphasis made of the importance of sexual chemistry. Before marriage a girl has to kiss a man to hold him, but after marriage she has to hold him to kiss him.

Don't underestimate this powerful connection either. When Cupid hits the mark he usually Mrs. it. Over the long haul of your married life, that's not enough energy to sustain itself. As terrific as pillowtalk is, it has to be backed up by kitchen talks and sofa talk, the "I'm home, honey" talk, daily-walking-together talk, or comfortable nontalk—seas of peace and quiet, sharing holy space. Just sexual attraction by itself wears thin very fast. Marriage is deeper than that, a communion of two spirits.

By this midmarriage stage, especially midlife stage, he should know by now your preferences. You should know his. It should be a mutual give and take. During this tough time for him, be full of praise. Compliment him during his trying sexual times. Tell him how good he makes you feel, that you love how he loves you.

Chief and I have always communicated easily through music. Look for it. For those who have responsive mates, scene setting becomes more important as your love life matures. It's more of a ritual, especially as your house empties of children. Then you don't have to grab sex wherever and whenever the two of you can. This is a great time for role changing, taking turns being the lover and the beloved.

If there's nothing going on, if your mate refuses to respond to any of your overtures, this is no time to overreact—to take it personally. Remember he's reached that point where he wouldn't be interested regardless of how well you present it. This is no time to test your attraction to the opposite sex other than your mate, or think you're "losing it." Be calm. Try to think of other ways, other things. Shift your drives into other directions.

Study, read, and learn. Eavesdrop with even greater intensity. Study your man with care. If he wants you to leave him alone, you must do so. This is no time to do anything rash. Remember your wedding vows. Try to remember "the way we were." Try to understand. Learn all you can about the male mid-life misery.

Women tend to read more, particularly psychological writings, trying to understand themselves, their children, and their husbands.

Men understandably tend to read more about their business and/or profession. You should know by now that when you married the man, you married the job. There may be times you allow yourself to think he loves his job more than he does you. That's infantile. He has to love his work to put up with the daily grind. If he doesn't love his work, now's the time to encourage him to launch into a second or third career. Finding fulfillment in his work, a sense of satisfaction, achievement is as important to him as being a good mother is to us.

Chief, a dentist, always notices teeth. He's more critical of mine. That doesn't mean he doesn't love me or that he loves dentistry more. If we go to the movies, he checks out the actors' teeth. It doesn't mean he doesn't love the theatre. He loves dentistry more. Men are like that.

A woman knows that the more she knows about herself, other women, and other men, as well as husbands, the better wife she'll be, a better-balanced person. Not only that, she's willing to share this knowledge. She feels almost compelled to do so.

They say men tend to read only about sports, politics, and business. Things related to their job. They're not into "why's." It doesn't occur to them to consider change. In fact they're afraid of change, generally speaking. They're really fatalists. They often don't want to know what causes heart attacks, for instance, or why they don't get along with others. Their theme song is, "I did it *my* way."

So knowing there's more truth than humor in "The only time you can change a man is when he's in diapers," what sort of attitude should a caring wife assume? Experts offer these suggestions to help the men in your life get through this dastardly decade:

- See it as a growth period, instead of a time of pain.
- Make it an opportunity for spiritual strengthening, reevaluation of the meaning of life as a couple.
- Be realistic about the number of pressures you're feeling. It may not be one major problem, but a number of small pressures building up that are causing trauma.
- Be willing to use outside help (clergy, counselor, therapist, psychologist) to help re-evaluate or set goals in life or marriage.
- Consider education, either a marriage course or participation in a marriage-communication encounter.

If there ever was a time to "stand by your man," this is it.

Wives, stay in prayer for courage, strength, and understanding to help you through this long haul. Try to restrain any impulses, anything stupid you might say or do. Don't do anything drastic or make any drastic changes either of you will regret later. Many a wife, if she doesn't get dumped during this period, dumps her "impossible" mate, then spends the rest of her life regretting the fact she didn't try harder to ride out this rough marital storm.

There's enough advice to go around concerning marriage for all of us to get more than our fair share. Oscar Wilde said, "All advice is bad and good advice is worse." Ruth Peale, wife of Norman Vincent Peale, in her book, *The Adventure of Being a Wife,* is one source of knowledge I treasure. This illustrious couple have had a long and happy life together. There's no reason the rest of us can't accomplish the same thing. I'm trying just like you are. If you are a mother, you understand the protective feeling you have toward your children. Remember your mate, like all of us, has the little "child" in him. So seeing your mate hurt or troubled or not himself for any reason should make the protective instinct run rampant. Why? Because your child is part of you. What affects him, affects you. So forget about wishing and wanting him to be a man. Just pray he will be.

Ruth Peale says she thinks this is the best epitaph a wife could hope for: "She was a wonderful shock absorber."

During this dastardly decade the secret of happiness is to learn to enjoy misery. It is a time your mate has "arrived." When he can be as cranky at the office as he is at the breakfast table. She doesn't wake up grumpy every morning, she lets him sleep.

You know your mate is in the murky waters of male menopause when complaints of his office tantrums reach you. They reach the point in their business or profession where they have "arrived." Feel like they don't have to prove anything to anybody. Willing to give ulcers, not get them, with no second thoughts or regrets.

Don't despair. Very often these attitudes, actions, and reactions that surface in your mate do just that—surface. Often strong and deep gratitude and affection are there, especially in those who realize "something's going on with me," who wonder if it could be the midlife crisis. But these grateful, affectionate feelings are buried so deep, no one can see them or feel them. Pity. The other spouse needs all the gratitude and affection she or he can get.

I believe the wife sets the emotional climate of the house. Never do you have to work at it any harder than during the middle years. The experts say "talk it out," but most men aren't geared that way. Chief isn't. No matter how I'd try to learn how to "talk it out" with him, I failed. It is a skill I've never mastered. He always took it as a danger signal, construed it to mean, "She's just trying to start something." My intent was to try to understand. I wanted to know how and why he felt and acted unlike himself. But since that was an impossibility, I tried to learn from "experts" about the mid-life crazies. I tried to filter through all the writings to see what applied, if at all, to Chief.

Chief vacillated between hot and cold—hot in temper, cold in actions. I hate to complain about Chief. After his stormy passage through the murky mid-life waters, he certainly has melted nicely.

Yes, it would be so much easier if your mate would allow you to try to soothe his hurt, if he could understand that wives are natural nurturers. Since Adam and Eve the wife has usually been the optimist of the family. Never is it more necessary than now.

Make a conscious effort to spoon feed all the upbeat news you can to him. I say spoon feed. There again, don't force feed him. Although you know he's in bad need of optimistic nourishment, he'd just spit it out.

I have a so-so record on this. Sometimes it helped. Most of the time Chief construed it to be idle chatter. Accuse me of saying things that were "irrelevant" or off the wall. Even though your intent might be to change the environmental climate—touch. The temptation to feel hurt, misunderstood, resentful, and to criticize is almost overwhelming. Try to conquer these feelings. Don't criticize. It's better to help your mate get on, than to tell him where to get off.

During Chief's "dissatisfied-with-everything" period, I was surrounded by children. So it was even more important I keep a loving, fun, optimistic environment. Even if I didn't always have Chief as a partner during those years, I stopped and thought. There are plenty of parents without partners. Concentrate on the children. Four had already left the nest. I still had one who was there throughout and old enough to understand. The last four needed all the love and nurturing I could give them. They needed to be taught, encouraged, and motivated. Motherhood is still the most important job in the world. It has to be done, with or without a partner.

My children were my joy, my sunshine, adding to the mirth of my marriage in an inevitable miserable stage. Chief is not my child. I am not his mother. All I could do was provide as loving, understanding, fun place to be "home" within my power from above.

The oldest child at home was high-school age. Those who had flown the coop were mostly unaware of the change in climate at Bedlam. Of course I honored not only Chief's public image but his image with his own family. I never played games with them. If they were old enough to understand and ask questions, I shared my newfound knowledge about male menopause with them. I talked with them about upholding Chief's public image also. I reminded them to keep enumerating his good qualities. He still had them. I reminded the older troops how lucky it was for us Chief didn't do anything really wild, weird, or sinful. He was a good man. He is still a good man. To cling to that. So he is impossible right now. Remember this, too, shall pass.

Thanks be to God we've lived long enough to see it. Thanks be to God, I had children who were understanding. I desperately needed their love. Number-three son, the peacemaker, wrote me a Mother's Day message I treasure. He recruited the others to sign it. Then once, when I was getting a little down with the situation, he surprised me with a public acknowledgement of my childrens' sentiments. He had a plaque made with "Our Mom, Libbylove, Mother of the Year, 1974 to Infinity. We love you." It was beautiful. At the time, I wished they had signed their given names. But now I treasure the fact, they were signed by their nicknames. I'll never forget those: "Mer, Buddy, Tooty-bug, T-Bone, Jepe, Hokie, Lip, Dude, and Bookie." When I say "public," this memento was presented to me at wedding-rehearsal dinner number four. The youngest wrote such a great Mother's Day letter for a local contest, he won me two new dresses. They gave me love and support.

How did the children cope, act, or react to their father's middle-life misery? They, too, fed him only positive things about themselves, their lives. They learned to let the negative things Chief said go in one ear and out the other. He became such a nag. He said the same negative thing to the same child so much I was afraid they wouldn't come back home. They each had their own way of coping as would be expected. They learned to listen as long as they could stand it. Always quiet and respect-ful. But they'd leave the scene as soon as possible.

Never would I attempt a conversation that could possibly be stressful to Chief. It wouldn't go round and round into the wee hours. Chief would cut you off pronto. Now maybe your mate is different in that department. I still have a few children who have difficulty talking with him although they want and need advice they feel only he can give. No, your mate is not interested in analysis of any kind, particularly his "problem," your problem, anyone's problem. You finally have to face it. *You are the problem.*

The children and I would laugh as to which one of us was *his* problem —the problem of the day. I won, hands down. All any of us had to do was listen to him. His theme song? "I tell them. I always tell them. But *nobody listens.*"

One of our family jokes, now that Chief has passed through the pivotal decade into the Mellow Age, is his famous statement, "If you don't think like I do, you're stupid!"

Chief has come a long way, baby. Even he can laugh at that statement, though he still believes it. To hear the other sons repeat it, innocently most times, brings gales of laughter. Cooking doesn't last. Good humor does.

9

Are You Living a Life of Quiet Desperation, or Are You Married?

Are you living a life of quiet desperation? Or are you married? The big question most husbands have to decide is: Are they a man or a spouse? Most weddings are double-ring ceremonies. One around the bride's finger and one through the groom's nose. That's why they say marriages are made in heaven, and Reno, Nevada, is where they're often called back for repairs.

According to some experts, the trouble with the world today is people are adding love to dog food when it's marriages that need it.

A domestic quarrel's when she says, "I'm so upset, I'm going to a headshrinker." And he says, "It ain't your head that needs shrinking—it's your mouth."

This is the kind of jokes making the rounds. Marriage is always picked on. Chief likes the one: A husband is a person who's under the impression he bosses the house when, in reality, he only houses the boss. This joke's special to me because Chief added these words, "if he loves her."

We both are bad about writing in books. We share joke books. He puts a *C* by those he likes. I put an *L*. It makes it more fun when I pick up a book and note what he thought was funny. We both feel stress is greatly relieved by humor.

It's said a marriage counselor believes the most foolish woman can manage a clever man. But it takes a very clever woman to manage a fool.

Why do we remain fools? Why don't we grow up? Mature? Begin to show some class? Maybe it's because we don't have the foggiest notion

what maturity means, what class is. It's sort of like tacky or treasure—
two views of the same thing.

This is my favorite definition, tattered and torn, that I've clung to:
class is being considerate of others. It knows that good manners are
nothing more than a series of pretty sacrifices. Class bespeaks an aristoc-
racy that has nothing to do with ancestors or money. The most affluent
blue blood can be totally without class, while the descendant of a coal
miner may ooze class from every pore. Class never tries to build itself
up by tearing others down. Class is already up and need not strive to look
better by making others look worse. Class can "walk with kings and keep
its virture and talk with crowds and keep the common touch." Everyone
is comfortable with the person who has class because he is comfortable
with himself. If you have class, you don't need much of anything else.
If you don't have class, no matter what else you have, it doesn't make
much difference.

I truly believe if we'd treat our spouses with a touch of class, we'd have
happier homes. Especially the class "that never tries to build itself up by
tearing others down. Class is already up and need not strive to look better
by making others look worse."

It's easy to catch the fever of marital discontent. It's contagious. It's
perfectly possible for your mate to catch it before you do. Chief did. We
all are on our own hormonal clock. Marital discontent is contagious.
Like the flu, you can catch it. That's what you have to guard against most
vigilantly.

One friend I talked with said, "My _____'s lethargy finally got to
me. I could see he was deliberately tuning me out. The only area where
he showed any emotion was sex. In every other way, we lost step. Fell
out of rhythm. I can't take that deadness anymore. His burnout or
mid-life behavior's becoming infectious, Libbylove. I'm sinking. Help!
Help! I want a divorce!"

"It can't be that bad. Don't be rash. Why would you consider divorce?"

"Libbylove, we have nothing in common anymore. We don't even hate
the same people!"

All I can do is be my friend's knee-buddy. We flop down on our knees and pray. I share some of my survival techniques, marital checklists. This knowledge I'm sharing with you. Why? In hopes you won't forget:

- This dastardly decade is not here to stay. It will go away.
- That you will be so glad you stayed. It is so well worth it.
- The best is yet to come. It's what it's all about—to become two mature people who still love, respect, and enjoy each other with the full knowledge, satisfaction, and fulfillment that they honored the covenant they vowed on their wedding day: never to let man, woman, business, sports, children, or the *dastardly decade* put us asunder. No, God joined us together. I'm glad. You will be, too, so hang in there.

A lot of good positive things can come from this stressful period.

You learn how to cope. You learn to get your own act together, your drives in other directions. That's not all bad. It's high time we all grew up, like everything else. It's more fun together.

The late Sydney J. Harris, one of my favorite writers, talked about our vision of situations. Everything depends on how you look at it. The difference in copers and those who break down in one way or another is all in how they look at things. Some slide into apathy, depression, self-destructive, or violent tendencies. The copers have a "normal ability to shift their points of vision." Harris gave examples of trick pictures so popular in the 1920s. Remember the picture of a couple kissing that slowly turns into a vase? Or the pretty girl who you finally see is a witch? It's all in how you look at it. So it is with our lives. So much depends on our vision, our point of view, mood.

We know we can help our mates most by helping ourselves. Interpersonal problems are rarely one-sided. When our spouses see us taking a constructive step, they may be encouraged to do something constructive, too, and not continue slipping down their self-destructive path. They might take responsibility for their own actions. It's certainly worth a try. Setting a good example for our children certainly is the most effective tool. Why wouldn't it work with our spouse?

If all we know is falling down around us, . . . we still know what we *should* do. (Remember, never compromise yourself or your principles.)

Getting our drives in the right direction will pay off, too. In a talk I give, "There Is Life After Children," I tell of my attempts of trying to get back into the swing of things after a thirty-four year period of raising children. I tell of my monumental failures and my miniscule successes.

A very funny thing happened while I was into this period of seeking new directions for my life. I was hotly pursuing writing. I took seven years of creative writing classes. This helped me through this dastardly decade. I also pursued a speaking career. Anyone with nine children has drive.

I was at a dental wives' luncheon at our state meeting. The speaker was a graphologist. All of us had to write a paragraph for her to analyze. All wrote the same assignment. It happened she picked up mine. Before over a hundred folks I knew, this monologue followed:

"This person, Libbylove, is not getting enough sexual satisfaction."

With this, the place went bananas with laughter. Thinking her word choice was not quite appropo, she carried on.

"You know what I mean, she's not getting *enough!*"

Her audience was falling out of their chairs by now. The speaker drew herself up erect, turned to the president, and said, "What is going on here? I'll have you all know I'm a certified graphologist! Certified witness at forgery trials. I am a serious professional. I have given this talk a thousand times. I have *never* gotten this reaction!"

"What you don't know is . . . this lady has *nine* children," the president said.

With this, the speaker turned on her heel towards me, pointed her long finger my way, shook it in front of my nose, and said, "What I'm telling you, Libbylove, is—*you need to get your drives in other directions.*"

I have. The very speaker who told the whole world about my sex life is now a good friend. I discovered she was a newspaper columnist. We went to a lot of meetings together after that. I was delighted to warn everybody about her, jokingly, of course, "She'll tell your secrets before everybody. Watch out."

Maybe the wish for change has been in our spouse's life for a long time. In middle-life menopausal period, the conflict becomes more visible. It doesn't have to be a signal or fear that a hidden battle will flare into open warfare. It could be instead, a period full of hope. At least you know what's ailing him.

When you have every assurance your beloved is in menopause, you've met the enemy. You can then decide how to do battle to survive, even if you can't help him through it.

My plan was to win through action rather than counteraction. No threats. No incriminations. Never frighten an egotist if you wish to win. Who knows what lurks in the menopausal mind if they don't say? Some wives are lucky enough to have a mate who will share his feelings, fears, and terrors with them. I just happen not to know any.

Be nonchalant. If insults, criticisms are thrown or you're the doll they stick pins in, don't swell up, strut like a peacock, or act self-righteous just because you've gained a little knowledge on the subject of male menopause.

Any man knows nothing makes a little knowledge so dangerous as thinking your wife doesn't have it.

Now if you think he's trying to deceive you (who knows?) or is playing games, keep your cool. Keep your evidences of power in the background, your steady, unflappable demeanor. Your faith that the dear Lord will see you through this mess is your hidden power. So never act like you're so good, so perfect, or crow about your patience and understanding. Most folks take warning from our thoughtless boasts. But they overplay themselves when we appear as little targets. They eat it up. The worse your trouble, experts tell us, the less your strength should be apparent. Only cowards shout and threaten. So don't play that game.

So it's your nature to apologize, to say you're sorry? This is no time for power plays. Although there are constant reminders of how dependent you really are, either financially or emotionally, you'll never know the power in another, not if you refuse to give this power an opportunity to express itself. Another's strength can't show if yours is running full speed ahead.

It's no time for recanting your own needs and weakness. His arrogance will appear. Only in this way, as I see it, can you learn to see and identify destructive qualities in him and in yourself.

In other words, innocent honesty is more powerful than most anything. Sheer simplicity is the greatest protection against duplicity. Most husbands don't fear those new gadgets that can tell when they're lying. They married one.

Chief was into flirting a little more than usual during this period. But he wasn't into infidelity. Was it because by the time he wanted to roam in those "green" pastures, he realized he couldn't jump the fence? No, like most of us, he has his faults. But infidelity isn't one of them. When one of my friend's wives was in her menopausal period, he said he wished she would find someone else. But lots of misunderstandings can arise. Foolish conduct and foolish things can be said. Flirting hasn't changed much in twenty-five hundred years. Greek girls sat and listened to a lyre all evening.

Many foolish wives think flirting is a sure sign of infidelity. Not so. Many see smoke where there's no fire. Let's face it, the man who flirts in the presence of his wife is not practicing for a full-time affair. Most men flirt to reassure themselves they're still attractive to the opposite sex.

There are always females lined up to play the game. I had a pact, my son number-four's idea. I would call him to come get me if I couldn't take this foolishness any longer. I called him once. It was a pretty good tolerance test, but there's nothing in the book that says you have to stay and watch. I do think a woman is foolish to accuse her husband of infidelity. If she does this enough she just might put the idea into his head. Her own jealousy might drive him to the very situation she feared most.

I think a wife would be rather insensitive if she didn't want other females to approve of her choice of a mate. I am proud, not jealous, even a little smug that other women find Chief attractive. I want other women to find him fun and attractive. I've spent many moments wondering what in the world attracted my friend to her husband. He has no personality, no charm, dullsville. Dumb? Money? Power? Last chance? It's a good thing we don't like the same things.

I've seen some men flirt to make their wives feel miserable. This type's not really interested in the other woman. They just get a sadistic satisfaction out of making their wives suffer. They know they can hurt, so they get that power going. A man never falls in love with a woman he understands, but with one who understands him.

As for jealousy, insecurity breeds it. Psychologists tell us this is another way men and women are different. When a woman's jealous, it has a lot of "fear" behind it, fear of being displaced.

Male jealousy is purely possessive. It has everything to do with sex. Just the idea that another man attracts his wife drives him practically crazy. I always felt I'd be one big fool to let Chief know what males I thought were attractive. A husband can talk about good-looking chicks all night. But a good wife only talks about handsome men around her girl friends. It's good common sense.

The trait of wanting to know if you're still attractive to the opposite sex is not limited to males. That's human nature.

Even the most perceptive women often miss significant clues to infidelity. If she wanted to know, there's plenty written on the subject about symptoms, supposed reasons. The truth is, most women really don't want to know.

When a person tries to fool themselves, their deception interferes with their own honesty. So be calm. He gets so mixed up in his own calculations he can't grasp your strength. This doesn't apply just to infidelity. It is true of any kind of deception.

Whether he's lying or cheating to himself, or to you, is his problem. If you're natural and ingenuous as a child, your directness puts him off. He expects confrontation, whether it's shouts, threats, or similar behavior.

Having two faces, he cannot look in one direction. "Treachery destroys the wits of the user" says an old adage. That's why a sly, manipulative mind never knows good strategy. It can't see beyond its own mischief. In the peaks of mid-life crazies, he could care less for consequences. Having no conscience—not being aware, he cannot, for the life of him, understand the sturdiness of yours.

They say only the monkey, besides mankind, lacks the intelligence to keep still. Your mate might blate. The monkey chatters before swinging on a vine. A cat, you'll notice, crouches before springing. Only the tip of her tail reveals her purpose. Even her switching is unwise—a giveaway.

Silence can work miracles. We know that through our prayer life. Vacuums are more powerful than wind. I can survive most any situation if I'm calm about it. Ask and receive His help. I'm not saying it's easy. I'm so excitable, I've always had to work at being calm. In raising my nine, I've been accused of being a calm person. But I'm like a duck, calm on the surface, but paddling like fury underneath. During this trying time, my vacation was a brief relief without the Chief.

If calm, I can make great progress. I try not to even attempt to clear up a bothersome, troubled situation when upset about it. I try to let it alone until I can see the funny side of it, even if it takes ten long years. It's worth it. If you draw away in foolish pride, it will still be a long ten years, a very long cold winter of your life.

Sure your beloved has become cold and aloof. Now you know why. Use a different "coals of fire" treatment, the thawing method. Although the results seem remote, build that fire. Fan that flame. Review the things he used to like. If you can't move an iceberg, melt it. It doesn't have to be a four-alarm fire. He'd flee for sure. Probably waiting for the slightest excuse. Don't you give him one.

Melting him will be fun, too, in time. Just keep shining on him with as much warmth as he can take. He hasn't a chance against our true, honest, radiant affection.

Although this is the method I chose, I wouldn't recommend it for everyone. Not if your *heart's* not in it. Don't practice this art of good nature. (It is an art—one I have to work at daily.) I do think you have to *honestly* feel this way. Try to discover what good nature is—how you honestly feel towards your mate.

I don't believe any "success books," how-tos of marriage, or any helps I might give you will work. Unless you have a realistic picture of your own unique situation, any advice will fail unless you sincerely feel what you do.

Often a husband wishes his wife hadn't said she'd given him the best years of her life. Now he's just as discouraged as she is. It's no wonder he has a thing about women during these years. The average man's life consists of twenty years having mom ask where he's going. For forty years a wife asks the same question. At the end the mourners are wondering, too.

Kathleen Norris, who wrote so many short stories that helped wives through trying times, thinks most divorced wives regret it.

But most of a divorcee's regrets were centered around simply missing him. She admitted she liked having a man around the house. I could identify with that. I get teased because I write on the bottom of toilet seats. After all, they're always up in my house. I might as well decorate them. The guest bathroom has, "It's so nice to have a man around the house." The toilet seat in our bathroom says, "A man in the house is worth two in the street."

A friend of mine said, "I like his racket in the hall when he gets home at night. I like him to pay my restaurant bill, and say 'How ya' fixed for money, Honey?' I like to fuss over him when he feels sick, and have him fuss over me when I do. I tell you, Libbylove, a little loneliness as a wife is better than total loneliness as an unattached female. A faulty human man, with 27 percent selfishness, is better than no man at all. I'd tell anybody who reads your book, Libbylove, that's even thinking about divorce—don't. I think I could have made it if I hadn't given up. Nine times out of ten I can see that our troubles were imaginary or certainly curable. If you get a divorce, you'll find out what real trouble is."

By the same token, four out of five couples would marry again. Happiness in marriage isn't due to easy finances, romantic lovemaking, marrying at a certain age. A long engagement. The most critical factor in "making a happy marriage" are the personalities of the husband and wife. Marriage is the extreme test of a person's ability to get along with others. It's usually the personality of husband or wife, not money or sex, that puts a strain on a marriage.

When your marriage hits this dastardly pivotal decade, hang in there. It could reach the peak we'd love, if we'd only watch our personality.

Here are some easily remembered C's of weathering this trying period covered in this chapter: *calmness, consideration, cooperation, conservatism, cleanliness.*

The only one of these traits I haven't commented on is conservatism.

I've read and studied it. Here are some things I really hadn't thought about, but observe to be true: People who are accused of being "agin' things" find happiness against them in marriage. Psychologists say if you're too radical in politics, unconventional in your life-style, and cynical about religion, don't expect too happy a married life.

The humdrum conservatives find married life happiest. They're made fun of by folks with "modern ideas." But conventional folk have the last laugh. They stay married longest and happiest. Why? Because thrift and working hard are two qualities we find in conservative folks.

A conservative person accepts the world as it is and makes the best of it. He stays in the middle of the road in his opinions, neither struggling to keep things from changing at one extreme, nor fighting to reform them at the other. Being conservative is a great personality goal for married happiness. Chances are you won't be the one who acts too hastily or do some wild, dumb thing during this wild, dumb time. No one will still be wondering what you'll be when you grow up.

10

How to Drive a Husband Crazy:
What Became of Mr. Right?

"You *never* tell me you love me," I said to Chief.

"I told you *once,*" was his quick reply. I looked at him. He was serious. "Let's get one thing straight. I'm *not* going through life saying 'I love you.'"

Those three little words were sarcastically delivered in a high-pitched voice. (Was he mimicking me? Did he think "I love you" is only said by females? I say, "I love you" almost as easily as I say, "Good morning." I say, "I love you" to those I love. I say, "Good morning" to everyone I meet.)

I whispered, "You're not?"

His eyes met mine. He was very serious.

"I come home every night. I bring you all my worldly goods. What more do you want? My life's blood?"

The subject was not brought up again. We had been married less than a year. I had just participated in a pasttime most wives are guilty of—a life-style: how to drive a husband crazy.

That was one of the first times I realized I drove my husband crazy asking silly questions. I was trying to get the hang of being a wife. When I concluded I wasn't doing very well, I wondered if he really was Mr. Right. Could I live without being told, "I love you"?

I learned a great truth. There are many many ways to say, "I love you." Actions do speak much louder than words. Chief was a man of action. I got the message. He loved me.

Not long after that, out slipped, "You *never* give me a compliment." We'd just finished dinner. I felt so good. I had at long last mastered a meal, one that came out right. That's when you remember to put the rice on first to boil. Then it will be done when the other vegetables are, like magic. The green beans almost tasted like his mom's—a miracle.

"I only tell you when you do things wrong, incorrectly. I *expect* you to do things right." I looked up. The tone was harsh. But, the look was pleasant. He had just stated a fact. No, his eyes weren't dancing. He wasn't kidding.

Once more I realized I had slipped, very innocently, into whine gear, participated in a pastime most wives are guilty of. I look at him, wondering, *What happened to Mr. Right? The gusher. The guy from whom compliments flowed like wine?*

His words woke me up. *Hey, I must have been dreaming. This is my husband. My friend who tells it like it is—according to Chief.* Yes, I was daydreaming. Remember those guys who wrote poetry to you; sang in your ear; wafted wolf whistles. Where did they all go? The one I dreamed would one day come along and win me? Tall dark and had some? I fell for a tall, blonde who had none.

I had no intentions of playing with fire. I knew I'd end up cooking over it. A girl will continue to string along with a guy just to see if he's fit to be tied. Where did they all go?

Momentarily, I missed my boyfriends. I looked up. There was Mr. Right who would become the father of my children—Chief of the clan. He smiled his snow-melting smile. He could make me forget all those gooey gushers. And he did.

Breaking the habit of compliment fishing was easy. I learned fast. The subject never came up again. I comforted myself with the thought, "Hey, I gotta' be good, I passed his test." I was getting the hang of trying *not* to drive my husband crazy. We agreed on the important things. I was trying to reach agreements on the unimportant things that become important if you let them. They're so daily. I had so much to learn, especially to drop the word *never* from my vocabulary. Never say *never* again. "You never say this," or "You never do that." *Never* was a culprit. I was always getting caught in my own mouthtrap.

When I married Chief, I lost a great friend, but I gained a great lover. After nearly five decades of marriage to this man, I have never regretted it. I've been momentarily disappointed, dismayed, dissatisfied, and disgusted, but I've never regretted it.

Sometimes he's my beloved. Sometimes he's my lover. Sometimes he's my buddy. He's always my friend. I love him dearly. Good friends never disappoint you or forsake you. I have been blessed with lots of female buddies, male friends, but only one lover—Chief. Not that I don't have a sense of adventure. I just think the adventure should be enjoyed only with the one who married you. My marriage is like that—an adventure in mirth and misery.

In mastering "how to not drive a husband crazy," I've learned to try harder, to add more fun to daily living, more mirth than misery to this adventure.

Before any adventure come high expectations. None are so great as in marriage. The danger of bringing unreal expectations to marriage is worth warning against couples repeatedly. Nothing is so blinding to this binding than excessive expectations.

Have you seen the cartoon of a girl talking to a marriage counselor? She says, "When I got married, I was looking for an ideal—then it became an ordeal—and now I want a new deal."

The things I say about marriage apply to both husband and wife. We're not really all that different. We're human beings first.

So many couples today come into matrimony with the "What's-in-it-for-me?" attitude. They are the get, get, get generation, not the give, give, give. As they say—don't give till it hurts, give till it feels good.

Plenty of mutual likes and dislikes surfaced during my seven-year friendship with Chief. We both like people, activity, and homemade ice cream. We both dislike extreme heights, severe lightning, and constant complainers.

Yet, we are two individuals. We have two ways of looking at the same thing—his and mine. These are not two different opposing points of view—male and female—but rather two ways of looking at the same thing.

After a few years of marriage, it's said a man can look right at a woman without seeing her, and a woman can see right through a man without looking at him.

Part of the adventure is learning to gain strength from each other's differences instead of letting them split us apart. One of the most celebrated, fascinating components of marriage is the differences between male and female.

The bra burners would have us believe there is *no* difference beyond the obvious physical ones. If true, why marry? Each sex looks at the world differently. A man, from his view, sees at best (according to male psychologists) only 50 percent of its richness and complexity. A woman? Probably 50 percent of its wonders and simplicity.

In addition to the "blessings and bothers of babies," another purpose of marriage is to share and enjoy our mate's differences. How many of us do that? Usually we criticize, have constant comments, or jokes that are strictly put-downs. Another purpose of marriage is to gain, from each other's weaknesses, a better, broader understanding of the world and all that's in it.

We certainly gain better understanding of ourselves than we could ever have on our own. When a man displays strength of character in his own home, it's called stubborness. Men learn more women have knowledge of parliamentary law than they first believed. Now they've seen them in office. It doesn't come as a surprise to most men. They'll tell you in a flash that their wife's been speaker of the house for years. If we weren't married, how in the world would we ever know our faults?

Margaret Thatcher's proved a woman can be an aggressive war leader. Golda Meir and Indira Gandhi's records show they have given or taken supreme power. We see that women use power about like men do in similar situations. Men can vouch women execs can hire, fire, and deal just as toughly with the best or worst of them.

When you marry one of these "modern" girls, remember, she knows all the answers before marriage. After marriage she's like most of the other wives. She knows all the questions. Never tell this liberal, educated type that you are unworthy of her. Let her find out for herself.

Women and men, given the right circumstances, can equal or excel one another physically and emotionally. Yet, very clearly, women are not men or vice versa and don't want to be. I had my doubts about one wedding Chief and I attended. Thirty minutes before the ceremony, the bride and groom were flipping a coin to see who got to wear the gown. I do think this is an exception.

Wanting the same advantages and opportunities is very different from wanting to be a man. Instead of trying to eliminate the difference, we would be better off learning from them. I've found I am always learning. He can point out logical reasons for me to do something differently. He's usually right, because he brings a different point of view. I not only enjoy a fresh viewpoint but sometimes it's cause for celebration. Chief even brings new ideas into the kitchen, now that he's learning to cook. I can learn from him, even after being his teacher.

The question of who'll check the car, or who'll do the dishes can be settled simply. They even have one of those sexy after-shave lotions called "Take Out the Garbage." You put it on and, five minutes later, they're all over you, not women—ants.

You know you're married when you see this fella in his slippers and bathrobe taking out the garbage on a cold rainy night. You recognize him. It's you. Garbage was no question in our house. I took it out if it bothered me. As we had more children and more garbage, we also had more garbage taker-outers. Now that there are the two of us, I still take it out if it bothers me. He does likewise. Between the two of us, it gets taken out. This is not like the woman who insisted her husband take the garbage out with her. She wanted the neighbors to see that he did take her somewhere. I never had that problem. Both people lovers, we go out. That trait's on my "plus" list.

No, the question isn't who does the dishes or look after the car. The question is, how will we look after each other? How will we look after our marriage?

Certainly one way is to try to avoid driving each other crazy. I can't repeat enough—*study your man*. Learn what makes him happy or unhappy.

Accept each other as he or she is. Accept each other's needs and viewpoints without compromising, sacrificing your own self. I didn't say it was easy. The framework of marriage may be made in heaven, but the details have to be worked out here. Our differences head the list.

It is said men like silence, think it is masculine. It is said women like silent men. They think they're listening! The truth is: one way to save face is to keep the cover half shut.

Chief is from a very verbal family of extremes. Some hardly ever say anything. Others talk all the time. Probably the quiet ones, like in any family, never have a chance. Even when they had words, some never got a chance to use theirs. Chief's family's no different from mine or anyone else's.

George Meredith said that woman will be the last thing civilized by man. The English equate civilized with having a way with words. Historically, women have had too many. In lots of civilizations, women could not enter conversations. That's still true in some countries. Women do talk with women and that's it.

I really think talking drives a man crazy, most of them. They love the beatitude that says, "Blessed are they who have nothing to say and cannot be persuaded to say it." I know one exception. I have a friend who wanted to go to the beach for the weekend. I happened to be drinking coffee in their kitchen. He turned to his wife, hand over the telephone, ready to make reservations for a place to stay. He said, "Sarah, are you going to talk to me?"

She said, "What do you mean, am I going to talk to you? I'm talking."

"No, I mean will you talk to me while I'm driving to the beach?"

Silence.

Then he looked at me, hand still over the mouthpiece of the phone, and said, "Sarah won't talk to me when we travel. She always sleeps. And I want somebody to talk to me. That's a long ride to the beach."

Sarah laughingly agreed to talk to her husband. He happily finished making arrangements.

Knowing when to talk and when not to talk is one of the first lessons in marriage. Sure you have times you'd like to talk. But go somewhere else. Find somebody else to talk to *if* it drives him crazy.

A man who's interested in marriage preservation, especially his, should set aside some time to talk and listen.

A woman who's interested in the same goal, should accept the fact there are times men simply have to get away by themselves, in some real or invented masculine pursuit—to be with the boys.

Luckily for me, Chief has time with the boys. He plays tennis and golf regularly. It makes him more content. He gets good exercise, too. He has always belonged to a civic club. Now he's active in serving on the board of trustees for our technical college as well as several other boards.

Remember, these are not two different opposing points of view—male and female. Some men like their wives to talk. It's just two ways of looking at the same thing, two ways of appreciating, two ways of expressing it.

Neither male or female has a monopoly on truth. We need one another. We deserve one another. Remember the beginning of life, without each other, would be impossible. The middle of life would be without pleasure, and the end without consolation.

Who started this battle of the sexes anyway? Why so much talk and print about who's better than whom? The anything-you-can-do-I-can-do-better attitude? I don't believe God started it. He didn't carefully, lovingly create Adam and Eve, present them to each other, and then stand back to watch them shoot each other down.

Today, bullets are flying, zings of all kinds. It's open warfare. Jokes abound about the opposite sex. Instead of cultivating a relaxed, good-natured, sense-of-humored relationship, it's one skirmish after another. The trend seems to be cultivating difference. Instead of striving to be sources of strength and fun, playmates and good buddies, differences are enthusiastically reported as pet peeves. There are those who seem to enjoy being on self-appointed fault-finding missions. They're having a heyday. It's the age of the put-downs. The supreme test of good manners is being able to put up with bad ones pleasantly.

For the first time in publishing history, a joke book was on the best-seller list. The title? *The World's Most Tasteless Jokes.* I saw an ad for the World's Ugliest Doll. It was horrible to look at. Foul language was programmed into it as were horrible smells from its mouth.

Personally, I believe in the hereafter. What I find hard to believe is the here and now.

Marriage has a hard time surviving in this negative world. Lest you think I'm trying to be Moses' replacement, let me be quick to remind you, I'm not that foolish. But I was foolish enough to chisel away on my own tablet, "Suggestions for Chief." No "Thou Shalt Nots" (I'm not crazy). But a list of "Oh, Honey, Please Don't Be Like Thats."

I hope you noticed I said these tablets were according to Libby, not Libbylove. Any person who tries to change another person is no love, believe me. It's not only foolish and potentially dangerous, it's downright impossible.

It's one thing to toy with eyeing Moses' job—big stuff on the mountaintop with the little ignoramuses below. But when you try to change another, you're messing with one of God's children. Then you're playing God. You don't want to start that. You're heading for trouble—big time. We're powerless. The only thing we can change is ourselves. We puny earthlings can't begin to do *that* without God's help.

Yeah, those tablets were too heavy and cumbersome. Slowly I learned to accept, adapt. I even learned to admire some of Chief's traits that once were pet peeves. I made such progress I whittled them down to rosary-size and put them away.

During his mid-life crisis, I pulled my rosary out like forbidden fruit to go over my pet peeves. Linus had his blanket. I had my rosary of Chief's habits that drove me wild: talking with his mouth full, and picking his teeth in public.

I thought of creative ways to alert Chief, particularly since habits are often unconsciously done. They'd have to be very creative. No one cares for criticism. I thought about blowing a whistle. That should get a response but was too risky. He never would let me use a whistle to get the troops in when they were little. I had to catch one and send him for the rest. I ruined my voice calling children.

I thought of putting on my wooden shoes he hates. I'd go clomping from room to room. I wear them for height. (My shoulders get tired from too-high counter tops.) The worse thing yet, is to mimic him, exaggerating his behavior, adding emphasis by making animal noises, or cracking jokes:

"I thought, during my freshman year at college, I learned a profound truth: from here on out, the person who picks up after me—is me. But I didn't learn the whole truth. During my freshman year of marriage, I learned the person who picks up after me—and you—is me.

"You have a wonderful way to make a long story short. You interrupt.

"You talk to your patients. You talk to your office staff. You talk to your golfing buddies. You talk to your car. You talk to other drivers. You even talk to yourself. Me you leave a note on the refrigerator."

When all else fails, there's nothing like using a few scare tactics: "I want to talk to you," or, "I'm gonna' tell your mama on you."

I try to be understanding. I've learned a lot about Chief. His glued-to-the-tube, fixed eyeballs, fingers tapping the end table, could mean he's thinking, not just addicted to television. Just because I prefer quiet thinking time doesn't mean a thing.

When I'm staring into space, don't throw the butterfly net over me. Or if you see me walking, driving, and talking to myself, Don't get the straitjacket. I'm thinking aloud, or practicing a talk. In these circumstances, I can finish a thought or a sentence uninterrupted. Not bad. We might not have any excuses for our behavior. But we have our reasons.

If your spouse has a habit you can't live with, suggest one you *can* live with—a substitute. For example, I suggested Chief could exchange his habit of buying four boxes of raisins when I just needed one for a habit of buying me a piece of jewelry every four years. Instead of making me cut his eyebrows—I like bushy eyebrows—once a week, he could substitute the habit of cooking dinner once a week.

To cool your anger, compare your mate's habits with others of the opposite sex you know. My friend did this very successfully. She was so annoyed by her husband's habit of idly scratching his chest as he lay next to her reading in bed until she remembered her first husband's habit of lying next to other women in bed.

Likewise, it bothers me no end that Chief rarely looks me in the eye when I'm talking to him—I made sure my children look you in the eye—until I remembered the boyfriend I once had who never took his eyes off me even to look at the road. It drove me bananas.

If there are truly awful habits you can't tolerate, you can always remove yourself. If it's nagging or a rehearsal of the same critical litany you've heard a million times, tune out, or take a self-hypnosis course. Walter Mitty and I are good buddies.

If every time your roommate blows his nose and it sounds like a bulldozer clearing land, there are ways to cope. Turn up the radio, or sing at the top of your voice. If you know this is dangerous behavior, perhaps it would be smarter to mentally transport yourself to some place more appealing.

We need to practice upping our tolerance level of our mate's habits. It's helped me to view Chief's habits as unconscious reactions to his environment rather than unconscious attacks on my sanity. It's a two-way street.

He cured me of poking him in the ribs. Watching movies, during our courting days, he poked me back so hard I almost fell out of my seat. It worked. Just maybe if I throw my pet-peeve rosary away, he'll feel like breaking the habit of never saying "I love you" in public.

Acceptance is made easier with humor. This little incident the children contributed. When they became old enough to see their parents' had habits for themselves, they began to mimic us. Behind our backs, of course.

I ran across this scene quite unexpectedly. We were vacationing at the beach. The younger children were teenagers and enjoying having teenage cousins to visit for the weekend. Their mother and I walked up on the porch, stepped back to view: To our amusement, my youngest daughter was wobbling into the room in high heels. Her usually cleanly-scrubbed face was caked with makeup. She had on a bright-colored dress and dangling earrings. As she made her way, precariously, across the room, she wore an exaggerated smile, with tightly clenched teeth. She never lost it. She'd dip and coo, pat or hug, each one in the room. Mimicking my syrupy voice, "Is everything all right? Did you have a good day today? Honey, you can do it. I just know you can do it."

I couldn't contain myself any longer. I started laughing out loud as she was laying one of my "I love you's" on one of their visiting cousins. They heard our laughs and made us come on into the house.

"Don't tell me I sound and act like that?"

"Oh, Mom, you all 'aint seen nothing yet!" they chorused.

In strutted son number six. He was tall enough now to wear one of Chief's wild sport jackets. As he strided across the room, he had an unlit cigar in his mouth. He was carrying a milk crate full of corn shucks. They bounced as he walked. He looked over the heads of those assembled until, on cue, a female voice chirped, "No, *not* more *corn!*" slinging her hand across her brow very dramatically.

The actor-son glared at the culprit, dropped the milk carton with a bang. There in the middle of the floor, he took his cigar out of his mouth, pretending he was spitting out little bits of tobacco. He lowered his head and gave everyone a drop-dead look. He turned on his feels and walked out.

The audience yelled and screamed its approval. I laughed in spite of myself. Remembering my mothering, I tried to chastise them, "You shouldn't make fun of your parents like that." Grinning, I added, "Dog-gone good performance though. You've got us pegged."

My niece nodded in laughing agreement. What could she say? She was the one whose mouth uttered the fateful words, "Not more corn." The scene was almost authentic except it was a crate of soft drinks that hit the floor. The unshucked corn came in bags. The teenagers wouldn't risk soft drinks, but they thought their performance was worth picking up the corn shucks.

Chief never saw that performance, but he enjoyed hearing about it. Now these scenes are part of our annual family get-togethers. Son number three does a great Cronkite imitation as he delivers a "State of the Family" address.

The use of humor can't be overemphasized. A family that prays together, we know, stays together. But a family that prays and laughs together has more fun.

11

How to Drive a Wife Crazy: Whatever Happened to the Girl I Married?

The woman lecturer was going strong. "For thousands of years women have been maligned and mistreated," she thundered. "They have suffered in a million ways. Is there any way that women have not suffered?"

As she paused to let that question sink in, a quiet, masculine voice answered: "Yes! They have never suffered in silence!"

This is one of Chief's favorite jokes. The second is like unto it:

Traffic cop: "I'm afraid your wife fell out of your car about a mile back."

Driver: "Thank goodness! I thought I'd gone deaf."

You can learn a lot about a man by the jokes he enjoys. I did. I gathered Chief thinks I talk too much. He gets such belly laughs when he tells these two pet jokes.

"Honey, do you think I talk too much?"

We were riding down the highway. I had my writing pad in hand.

"No. Why do you ask?"

"I want to get some input from you for *The Mirth and Misery of Marriage.*"

"Well, you know writing's *your* thing."

"Yes, but I wrote a chapter on your traits and habits that drive me crazy but are part of our marriage. You need equal time. Do you think I talk too much?"

"No," Chief laughed. "You don't talk too much. Like a lot of women I know, but I don't like it when you talk just to make conversation that's not even relevant . . . in public. Something to keep the conversation going. It's a family trait."

"How do you cope with this?" I asked, all ears.

"I just listen and say to myself, *This, too, shall pass.*"

That's exactly the way I deal with daily differences. I remind myself, "This, too, shall pass."

I kept quiet. Thought about my "keeping conversations going." *Must be my hotel upbringing,* I thought. *Conversation flowed freely.* When we are in a large crowd, I usually float on off to somewhere else in the room. I think most couples in midmarriage do this. You figure your husband has heard all you have to say, so you look for greener conversational pastures. Besides, Chief and I both are verbal. In his family, they have to be the dominant one or they walk away. I usually beat him to it.

That's what's nice about being married for awhile. It doesn't cause any concern to either spouse. In a small group, I can stick around and hear the same stories with the best of them. I enjoy hearing a good story again.

I admit if I think the conversation is negative, critical, or about to erupt into real unpleasantness, I say something "off the wall." I had a friend who delighted me with this trait. When the conversation became much too serious or totally boring he would ask, "What brand of toothpaste do you use? I use _____." Everyone would stop, forget the point they were going to make in the about-to-flame-up conversation. There would be a puzzled look on each face. _____? Whoever heard of _____? My friend assumed a totally innocent look on his face. So sweet and precious even other males couldn't become mad.

Sometimes I do that. Or sometimes I just say something stupid. Usually I try to fit the ploy with the group. I admit I'd rather engage in interesting conversation with people than merely be entertained. A spectator. I'm not talking about a monologue, which some people mistake for dialogue.

Yes, I thought to myself, *I must be more careful in conversation.* Then I asked Chief, "Is there anything else about talking you want to share with me? One of your pet peeves? I know you accuse me of mumbling. Don't talk loud enough."

"Oh, yeah, can't stand your mumbling. Speak up so I can hear you.

You know it drives me crazy for you to talk to me when I'm in another room. I don't know if you're saying something important. I don't want to miss it. Or if you're just talking to yourself."

I gave that some thought. I know why I mumble. It's sort of like testing the waters, saying, "Is this a good time to talk?" Also, I really can't stand loud voices. Particularly abrasive in females, I think. Sometimes I mumble when I'm tired, I notice.

Really, Chief has a point about talking to him when he's in another room. Guilty. It usually starts off with my trying to say something and he's walking out of the room. Or when I'm too lazy to get up from my typewriter and go ask, I am guilty.

"You're so right. I am guilty of talking when you're in another room. And I really don't know why I do it."

Silence.

"I must not be the only person who does it. Remember there was a play on Broadway titled, 'You Know I Can't Hear You with the Water Running.' "

"H-rummph."

"How about the little daily irritants, like . . . oh, I know, if I leave or anybody in the house leaves any liquid in their glass or cup, you come unglued. How do you feel about that? How do you cope with it? I just throw it out and wash the cup."

"Yeah, I think, *Why waste? Why get change for a dollar, spend like eighty cents wisely and then throw the rest away?* I take out what I want and drink it. Leave the rest."

"What about looks? I notice all the jokebooks have tons of jokes about a wife's appearance. I know it annoys you if eye makeup cakes in the corner of my eyes."

"Yeah, I don't like that, and I tell you. I doubt if you can see it. No, you're usually neat and well-groomed. No problem there."

"Thanks, I do appreciate your telling me if something isn't quite right about my looks. I know another thing you can't stand." I wrote notes as fast as I could. I know a man doesn't like to be questioned. But after all, this was one of his favorite subjects—me. "You don't like to have to wait on me to get ready."

"You're right about that. You usually ask me what takeoff time is and I try to let you know, so you will be ready."

"Anything else? What about when we disagree?"

"On a daily basis, you're easy to live with. Don't create any problems. You don't get mad often but when you do, boy! Then you save and bring them out one at a time. Then go back and enumerate all the things I've done you don't like. It hurts. Why bring up history? Something not relevant to the present situation? Especially when I don't see any reason. You lead me into false security. Open the floodgates and I wonder why. If I had known it earlier, I might have done something about it then. Makes me want to say, 'To heck with it.' Why should I exist if I'm making you that miserable?"

You know the end of that scenario. It's my job to admit that's the kind of temper I have. And to thank God I don't do anything worse. Believe me, I never deliberately try to make Chief mad. We ride along in silence. I can tell he feels better by having let me know. This was progress. Usually he lets me know what he doesn't like about me when he's angry or irritated. But to cooly, calmly tell me was something I could comprehend and hopefully do something about. When voices are raised, or angry, abrasive tones of voice used, it interferes with my logic. We both feel better. I chance talking.

"I made a list of the things I like about you. I think dealing with pet peeves is necessary. How to deal with them. But. I also think we ought to cling to what we like about each other."

"Get your pad back out. Here are some," Chief said.

- Your appearance is usually neat and well-groomed.
- You can go into most any situation and adapt to any situation very favorably. That I enjoy taking you.
- You get along with people. I'm happy to have you with me with any group of people.
- You're fun to be with. Can discuss anything—sports, religion, politics, marriage, family, education.
- I like your cooking and gardening.
- Your character is top grade—impeccable.

- You like most everyone except me at times. (We'd just had a great "discussion.")
- You're not a gossipy, critical person.
- You're most positive most of the time.
- You're negative to me on occasions by enumerating my shortcomings (!)
- You will not take advantage of another person but will help if you can.
- You basically try to live The Golden Rule.

As you can tell by the great dialogue, we had just had a great "discussion" the night before. So it was great to test some of my theories and things I had shared with you in previous chapters. Especially about anger. Interestingly we both agreed on the type I have. Did not agree on the type he has. Don't you think that's pretty typical? I do. Two ways looking at the same thing.

Like most married couples, we can quarrel. But it never affects the deep love we feel for each other. The many reasons and blessings we have accumulated over the years strengthen our marriage. We are partners without either of us losing our identity.

We are still friends. Our love is still full of tenderness, caring, understanding and passion in spite of the misunderstandings.

As for Chief, he still makes me like these things about him:

- The way he loves me.
- The way he lets me be me.
- The way he lets me do my thing.
- The way he's so generous to me and to others.
- I like his empathy, sympathy towards others.
- I like his participation in civic projects for the common good.
- I like his participation in and love of sports.
- I like his participation in and love for politics and his country.
- I like his participation in church and all its activities.
- I like the way he loves and continues to support me and our children.
- I like his ebullient personality.

- I like his quick wit.
- I like his ability to entertain and be the life of the party.
- I like his warmth, making an electric blanket unnecessary.
- I like his hands and the way he moves.
- I like the way he thinks things through.
- I like his practical and responsible attitude toward life.

We've been through a lot together. He's been through a lot with me. I appreciate his learning to rise above petty exasperations. I appreciate his dependability, loyalty, and mellowing with the years. No one can appreciate the delicate balancing of mirth and misery in marriage unless you've experienced it. It's so worth it. Yet, we are human. Either spouse at one time or another thinks he or she alone has the key to a happy marriage. It takes two.

I asked Chief to share some of his philosophy of marriage, too. He, too, like myself, is limited in his experience. I'm his first bride. But much-married Artie Shaw would have a different view. He probably wouldn't have time to write about it.

Here's Chief: "To make marriage work, both spouses have to be truly unselfish. And should have a desire to do everything within their power to make their partner happy. Instead of thinking only of me—satisfying me. Myself.

"For example, trying to arrange things you'd enjoy doing together to helping out with household chores. Being complimentary. To share love, ideas, as well as finances.

"A spoiled and inconsiderate person normally will end up in a divorce. A marriage should be with your eyes wide open before and half closed afterwards in order to be happy.

"Do not be picky about every little fault your mate has because both of us have faults. Pray to God you can overlook your spouse's faults and improve your own.

"You should have a lot of common interests. If you can't enjoy doing things together, it will be a boring marriage.

"If you don't enjoy talking to your mate before marriage, it is doomed to failure from the beginning. Have those communicating skills before and after marriage.

"I think one important prerequisite to a happy marriage would have a mutual interest in and love for God and the religious faith of your choice. That's the basis or foundation of a long and happy marriage.

"If both parties feel this way then the many obstacles of marriage may be overcome by prayer—praying together and individually.

"Marriage is like playing sports. Every day you will not be a winner. But every day will be a game. You can't win them all. One has to expect this but try to make the next day a winner.

"I think participation in sports as a child can teach a person how to live a happier married life. Because a person should not crow when you win. Or cry when you lose.

"Miracles can happen if a person can accept change. A person must be able to accept change in order to continue to be happily married.

"As we grow older, our body changes. We have to be able to accept that. And our situations change. That's life."

We rode down the road in silence. I thought of some wise words I'd heard, that

coming together is a beginning; keeping together is progress; working together is success. Success simmers down to this: making the most of what you are with what you've got. The trouble with too many of us is that in trying times we quit trying.

I wasn't about to quit trying. To be able to be together like this and tell each other what drives each other crazy was not only a beginning, but progress. Snap judgements have a way of becoming unfastened. I had really made snap judgments during our married life. Mainly because I was guilty of trying to read Chief's mind. We weren't giving each other clear information.

Trying to read your mate's mind is a foolish thing. We start by doing a lot of foolish things just for fun, and later they turn up as habits we can't shake. I really didn't try to read his mind just for fun. It was a necessity. Brought on by two extremes. One was silence. Chief's prone to periods of great silence.

Any man who works with people all day certainly needs silence. I respect that. Working with people is one thing. Working *on* people is another. Chief did both. Then, any father of nine children needs all the silence he can find. 'Tis said, "People who think too little usually talk too much." Chief used these quiet times to think. I respect that. I find no fault with that. I need silence, too. But the other extreme is saying, "I don't know what you're talking about." Or. "You don't remember I said that?" This drives you to mind-reading.

I long ago used my reporter's skill of writing down exactly what I hear. And hoping it was what was said. Your chances are greater if it is correct information. There are times in any relationship when you need correct information, or at least information.

You learn to smell a delay tactic. Hating to make decisions, Chief doesn't like to be tied down. He's found it's much better to say, "Anything you want to do." Or, "Anything you say." Then if it turns out to be a flop or he doesn't enjoy it, it isn't *his* fault. It was *your* decision. Now, that's a good ploy.

For a man who doesn't like to be tied down, Chief was in a real bind. Having been brought up in a male world, I knew they didn't like the third degree. To be questioned. Especially, "Where have you been?" Patience, my dear, in time he'll tell you. Most of the time gladly. If not, don't worry, the truth wins out. So don't make a federal case of every little thing.

Sure, you remember not to groan and whine. Let your home be a place he can rest easy. All well and good.

But.

There comes a time when you need some straight information.

You thought men always give straight information. Straight answers? That's a myth. No, the gender of a person has nothing to do with it. I had times I had to figure out if I was being fed baloney or blarney. Other times, it's like trying to pry a bit of information, like trying to pull eye teeth. Trying to read another person's mind for some clear information isn't easy. I want to say, "Stop, you're driving me crazy." And I'm sure Chief must feel the same way.

This was such a problem, I read up on everything I could on the subject. The psychologist called it "crazymaking." Here is what I learned to do:

1. Stop. Look. Listen. Feel. What is wanted of me?
2. Beware of crazymaking conditions. No need to guess. Assume about other's feelings. Examine your own feelings.
   a. Crazymaking's more likely when denied an open expression of wishes for *change*.
   b. Happens when one feels a sense of powerlessness.
   c. When felt, an open demand for change may result in *total* rejection.
3. Do not react blindly to the sting. Think and realize the other wants *change*. So bring it out into the open.
4. Respect other's rights to sanity. *Respond only to open communications.*
5. When in doubt (whether it's bait or truth), ask for the clear info you want.
6. In asking for clear information, confine yourself to matters that are open and immediate.
7. To obtain clear information about another's feeling, *share your own*. Don't introduce too many ideas and complaints. Narrow it down.

We have a right to our own sanity. Without it we are no good for anything or anybody. So living life well, fully as the dear Lord intended, is not one of wisdom only, but of daring. God will look us over, not for medals, diplomas, or degrees, but for scars. We may have the intelligence to see a practical solution to our marital problems, But do we have the nerve to follow up on it? If not, we might as well be stupid.

Providentially, I ran across the above food for thought. With lots of prayer, I followed these suggestions. Maybe you can get clear information from your mate. Don't need this. Great.

But. All of us have to decide what's right for us. Only we can decide.

There's no right and wrong in handling any problem until we decide what's right for us. The first step to consider is the consequences. Only then can we come to a definite decision as to where we stand. Then act. This worked for me.

But don't follow any advice, no matter how good, until you feel as deeply in your spirit—as you think in your mind. As in any daily quandry, ask and you will receive.

Don't waste time fretting and worrying about the future. Do what you know you ought to do today. The rest is God's affair. He has promised to be with us all the way. What more can we ask? Failure is doing nothing. The business of building a happy married life is the most important business in any person's life.

Not receiving clear information can create many unnecessary tensions and difficulties in marriage and in family life. Many tensions and difficulties arise in our ordinary, daily family routine. A great sense of humor can take the edge off of many bickerings and disputes that inevitably arise.

A good laugh can often clear the air. Many family problems are over minor items in the first place. Families who have a habit of integrating goodwill and humor into their family life suffer few conflicts and tensions. A hearty laugh and a sunny smile combine into the cheapest medicine known.

A warning: think, Ask yourself, "Do we use humor with care?" A joke, a witty remark, a mimic might relieve tensions in spousal spats. But don't use criticism to become a stand-up comic. Never try the funny-guy-or-gal routine by criticizing your spouse. For example:

"You know honey, I've just got to brag on you a little bit."

You're setting her up for a compliment. She's ready to breathe in some rare, sweet air. Waiting. Love in her eyes.

"You're about to get the hang of being a sex-pot."

She smiles. But. With a puzzled look. She wonders, *are you crazymaking?* She knows you look at sex-pots. But she thinks you don't want *her* to look like one. Who knows, maybe you're asking for "change." She's heard of the midlife crazies. She wonders, what *do* you want? But ever hopeful, grateful for a kind word, she waits. Then you lower the boom.

"Oh yes, dear. You're halfway there. You've got the pot and are working on the rest."

You lost her right after the reference to her midriff. She never heard another word. She never heard you give her credit for trying (if indeed, that was your intent).

This scenario might be funny to you. But not your wife. You can kid about a lot of things she'll be a good sport about. Her appearance. Her cooking. Her housekeeping. But not about her sex life. That is sacred ground. A heart-to-heart with love is the only method of delivery. Not humor.

How would you like it if she said to you, "Tell me, dear. Before we got married, did you say you were oversexed or over sex?"

The Golden Rule applies in marriage as well as life.

Humor gives us choices. We all love choices. In raising my nine, I had the choice of laughing or crying. We all have this choice. I choose laughing. And an appropriate joke allows those involved enough time to stop, rethink a position, or reconsider an action.

Even when feelings are at fur-flying pitch, a "Smile when you say that, podner," delivered with a big smile is a signal the door's not closed to further discussion. We need discussion in families. We need an open-door policy. Humor can open them easily. It reveals our humanness to our children. That as humans we disagree. But we can kiss and make up. Not silent. Smouldering. Certain we deserve better treatment.

Either spouse at one time or another thinks they deserve better treatment. Isn't that true? But stop and think. If we are treated less importantly than we expect, what are we saying? If not saying outright, we are at least implying that we deserve better. Deserve more.

How did Jesus act when slighted? He *humbled* Himself. He offered to serve. With a good spirit. He never insisted on preferred treatment. Going First Class. Treated like Royalty. Even though He *deserved* it. People owe us no special treatment (that includes spouses). But we owe God *everything!*

12

Grown and Gone:
We're Free at Last

It was June—when two-million graduates, including our last child, left college to look for jobs. Our number-nine child, number-seven son, who is one in a million, was one of those two million.

I looked at Chief. What could be going through his mind? Relief. He had just finished paying for forty-two years of college tuitions. I thought he looked pretty good considering he suffers from mal-tuition.

His physique, like the stockmarket, was all there, but lower. And I don't care what you say about baldness, I think it's neat.

Me? By the time number nine graduated, I didn't have to own antiques to sit down on something that was sixty years old. I was sixty-one. I was still a go-getter. Now it just takes me two trips. I've noticed I'm getting a double chin since I've been doing so much writing. I think it was just too much work for one.

We felt proud that seven out of nine had their college diplomas. The other two were late educational bloomers. But better late than never. They made it. Now we all had an education—a technique to open our minds, enabling us to go from cocksure ignorance to thoughtful uncertainty.

Back at Bedlam, the realization hit us. Hey, baby, they're grown and gone. Free at last! We looked at one another. We hugged one another. We kissed. We whistled and yelled. We saluted each other. We welcomed ourselves to a new adventure.

After plenty of thank you's to the One "from whom all blessings flow," we counted our blessings one by one. We had each other. We had our health. We have been blessed with nine lovely, healthy, good children.

We still like each other. We still love each other. We could still communicate. We're even on listening terms with each other.

There have been plenty of changes other than physical. At least we're more into changing ourselves. Our attitudes. Our hangups. Less with trying to change each other. We now know better. Realize God made us like He wanted us. We are learning more and more to accept and appreciate each other.

According to pop psychologists, in the children-grown-and-gone stage, it's the father who suffers more. Moms were thought to be devastated by the empty-nest syndrome. A California survey interviewing 160 women all but one responded to children's departure with relief.

Their husbands were full of regret. They look around and say, "Hey, where did they all go?" This is the same group of fathers who were too busy making a living. They had little time for their children when they were growing up. Not much interest in them. But when the kids were ready to fly the coop, dad was full of regret. They realized too late they had cheated themselves. Had not made time to enjoy the children growing up. Almost strangers. When they wanted to get closer to them, the children had no desire. Yet, when they were tiny tots, they begged and wheedled to get their fathers to do things with them.

All of these varied reactions to gone-and-grown depend on the husband's upbringing. Chief's father didn't do things with him on a regular basis. His philosophy? "Children don't want a pal. They want a father."

Chief adopted that theory. Although Chief plays sports, he didn't teach them. He was most happy to take them to ballgames. We had many happy years going to sporting events as a family. To this day, it's one of our fun things. Six out of the nine children live in our town. Most years we get a block of seats together. Other years we are scattered, but swap around, exchanging seats, to visit. This way it allows you the freedom of choice. To be with family. Or to get away with friends. Either way, there are no hard feelings.

These Saturday gatherings are a tradition during football season, particularly. We Southerners take our sports seriously. In fact, I tell my speaking audiences that in our family we don't dare get born, get married, die, or get buried without first checking the Atlantic Coast Conference Schedule.

When the nine were growing up, I always had a big pot of homemade chili on the stove. Out-of-town friends knew it. It wasn't unusual to have eight or ten extras come by. During the children's college years, bowls of chili were enjoyed by them with their welcomed friends. Bedlam's never been too small for our friends.

Now that the children are grown and gone, Chief has taken over the chili-making tradition. Instead of coming by before the games, those who can't come by after the game. They know the pot'll be on the stove all day. Like a lot of things, chili improves with time.

Tailgating before the game has grown in popularity. But the big pot of chili is still a Saturday tradition during football season. Now it's dubbed "Chief's Chili." It has won a chili cookoff contest. It's fed many church suppers and is sold at our church May Fair. As I told my friend, Maisie, when she was watching Chief wash up the big canning pots after cooking chili, "If you go about it the right way, you can take a lot of drudgery out of housework."

Chief and I are into role swapping now. I've been teaching him through the years to cook. It makes sense to me that when you like to eat, you ought to like to cook. Besides, what's a man going to do when it's too rainy to play golf? Fortunately, we live in the sunny South. So we don't have many days when you can't enjoy the outdoors.

Would you believe the first dish Chief cooked was shrimp creole? Ordinarily I wouldn't teach a rank beginner that dish. But Chief's not an ordinary sort of guy. I was home from the hospital with baby number nine. Chief not only wanted shrimp creole, he wanted to have some friends in to help him enjoy it.

Having babies was no big deal by then, as you can tell. I had enjoyed a whole week's rest in the hospital. There were plenty of children around to help. Even teens, if you could catch them.

"Just tell me what to do," Chief said. He had found the recipe. Gotten some of the troops to help peel the shrimp. He had put it all together before three couples in the neighborhood came. I was stretched out on the sofa, my newborn asleep in the upstairs nursery. The intercom was on so I could pick up any sounds. My own intercom was on. One ear listening upstairs, the other listening to the happy hubbub of my family and friends. I enjoyed it.

When guests arrived, they pitched in. Some visited with me. Others set the table, blending in with the busy children. Bouncing Bedlam.

"Where're your aprons?" a friend asked.

"Don't have any," I laughed. "I just take off my good clothes and slip into my cooking clothes when I cook." I looked at my well-groomed neighbor. It was very clear none of them could make it through all those children, pots, and pans without an apron.

"Look in my closet, there are enough maternity tops to outfit all of you."

With lots of laughs from their husbands and giggles from my crew, they had a great time that evening. All except one. One of the men, unlike the others, had never been to Bedlam before. His wife had but this was a new experience for him. He sat in the wing chair opposite me. Quiet. As if in shock. I enjoyed watching him watching the crazies roaming in and out of the room. He never left his chair until they called him to dinner. It didn't bother the other guys. They didn't invite him into the den with them. The poor man didn't know there was a haven of a den he could have escaped to. Just the thought of walking through Bedlam's kitchen to it was too traumatic for him to consider. He did make it the short distance to the dining room.

Chief's shrimp creole was delicious. But with all the hubbub of that memorable meal, I never thought he'd cook anytime soon. That was in September. In December we had a spell of bad weather. Chief asked me to teach him how to make vegetable soup. I'm the "just-throw-any-and-every-leftover-in-a-pot-with-a-little-meat-a-few-spices-and-lots-of-water-and-cook-and-cook" type. That didn't satisfy him. At his insistence, I measured and recorded each ingredient precisely.

With each success, Chief's confidence grew. By the time the grown-and-gone stage was upon us, I was ready to resign my job. Chief could take over. I passed my chef's cap to Chief. He now cooks chili and vegetable soup lots better than I do. He has even mastered the Southerner's delight, Brunswick stew. He uses his mother's recipe. He and his two sisters watched her make it. They wrote down exactly what she did as well as what she put into it.

His mother always made tons of Brunswick stew every Christmas Day. All her children and their families could go by whenever convenient. Since her death, Chief and his sisters make a batch together, carrying on her tradition.

Cooking with Chief is one of the fun grown-and-gone activities. Unspoken rules have come into being. Whenever one of us cooks, the other usually stays out of the kitchen unless invited. When Chief cooks chili, I open the canned goods. When he cooks soup, I usually locate and line up the spices for him. I cook and shred the three kinds of meat for his Brunswick stew. It matters not who cooks, the other doesn't question whether something is really "done" or suggest it needs salt.

We don't salt. Just keep shakers on the table. These may sound like small things to worry about. But we plan to be together a lifetime. Nightly second-guessing or unsolicited constant comments can drive you insane.

We're getting the hang of being alone—at last. We discovered we had more sofas and chairs than we thought. We could tell. There were no teenagers draped over them. New rules crop up everyday. I went into the kitchen for an apple to munch while we were watching Atlanta Braves. Without thinking, I had vacated the best spot in the house. An old, long, low-slung, over-stuffed couch. So low, it's a pain to get up from. We inherited it from Chief's older brother.

I knew all along the couch is the nicest place imaginable to watch the tube. Its goosedown pillows, soft and warm, make it the greatest place to rest your eyes and your frame. Especially if the ballgame's getting boring.

Chief had never even liked the couch. When I got back into the room, Chief was stretched out, even had pulled an afghan over himself. He was snug as a bug.

My protest, "That couch is mine. You never sit on it," went unnoticed.

"You didn't say a word about saving it," he grinned. "How did I know you weren't going out to stuff the washing machine?"

Of course, he didn't hold out. I sat on him pretending he wasn't there.

But from that night on, I realized I had inherited his wingback chair. And he has dibs on the sofa.

I had never thought much about these kinds of rules of marriage. When you think about it, animals have their territorial rights. With the nine gone, we had more territory to stake out. I know his nests and he knows mine. We don't touch. Some unspoken rules are rinky-dink. But they still throw a protective covering over our personal rights that make for a healthier marriage over the long haul.

Each partnership starts off with a few common-sense rules. Manners, which are nothing except consideration for others, cannot be overemphasized. Manners are that elusive quality you wish other people had—that you're sure you do.

It's against the rules to constantly interrupt. To break in on another's story. So many spouses have the self-appointed, "Let's keep the record straight, mate." You're familiar with the dialogue.

"We left about the middle of July."

"No, dear, it actually was the twenty-seventh of July."

"Okay, so we left on the twenty-seventh for Phoenix."

"No, dear, the tickets *said* Phoenix but . . .," he turns to your friends and says, ". . . but we actually went to Scottsdale. That's where the meeting was."

Get the picture? Chief's overlistening. Not because he wants to hear what I'm saying. He wants to keep the record straight.

I plead guilty to the "out-guesser" type. Chief does 90 percent of the grocery shopping in the grown-and-gone stage. This releases me of a thirty-four-year duty. He is a grocery-store graduate. Worked in one all through high school and college. He was house manager of his fraternity. He bought and planned meals for sixty boys. So he loves going to the grocery store now. It's like a family reunion. A homecoming. I wouldn't want to deprive him of the pleasure. He uses coupons. Shops for bargains. Still buys in great quantities. Like we still have a fraternity of our own.

"Libbylove, I was at the store today . . ."

"Don't tell me you bought another case of tomatoes?"

"No, I wasn't going to tell you that. I said I went to the store today and I saw Ernestine . . ."

"You saw Ernestine? How's she doing? Do her scars show? You know she had a face . . ."

"No, I did not see Ernestine Sawyer. I saw Ernestine Edwards. As I was trying to say . . ."

Or what about the "cross-examiner?"

"I met two cute girls at the luncheon today. We had a good time talking."

"Where were they from?"

"I don't know."

"What school did they finish?"

"I don't know."

"Well, for heaven's sake, what do their husbands do?"

"I don't know."

"Didn't do you much good to meet them did it, if you didn't learn anymore than that!"

"I just can't ask personal questions like that. All I know is they like Mobile. You remember Mobile? We were stationed there during World War II. Their husbands were, too. They like being mothers. They like North Carolina. As to how much their husbands make and all that, I don't ask."

Because an interview is easy for me as a newspaper person, you'd think I could ask personal questions. I can—with the person's permission. I've learned some people are super sensitive. Especially when questioned about their education, jobs, and so forth. Don't mind in my work, they expect it. I like a natural unfolding or sharing, if there's time. I have no hesitancy to ask people what they enjoy or are interested in. Chief learns more about people more quickly than I do. We just learn different things. That same two views of the same thing. Neither of us are real cross-examiners. I know some.

"Libbylove and I saw two of the prettiest deer yesterday. Didn't want to see them this way. They jumped over the engine of our car. We were driving to the beach. Don't know how they could have missed us. Scared us to death."

"Well, what kind of deer were they? Mule or Whitetail?"

"Gee, I don't know. They were in flight!"

"You don't know? Don't you know the difference? Well, in order to tell the difference you. . . ."

A scenario like this makes you wish you'd never mentioned the deer. Certainly not to your cross-examining friend.

These are just a few problems we run into in our marriage—from overlistening or non-listening. You don't mind seeing a couple that still cling like dust balls but break into each other's stories. Even if they brag about their charmed life, perfect marriage, and all that. But after the goo-goo-eyes stage is past, you can see the good fellowship fade. Then you hear, "Would you let me finish a story just once, dear." Or, "But you're missing the main punch line. The punch line is. . . ."

Don't panic. It's not even cause for alarm.

It's just another stage of love and marriage. Love is still there. Stop. Look. Listen. Even if you can't see it doesn't mean it's gone, just submerged. Just like the boss's wife told the cute wife of his young assistant —there was a lot of good in her husband. The young assistant's wife said, "Oh, Mrs. _____, what a sweet thing to say," to which Mrs. _____ told the young wife she was sure there was because he hadn't let it all out.

Most couples settle into a second stage of marriage very contentedly. They can feel the heartbeat of love. See flashes of it as they exchange glances across the room. Share a good laugh about their foibles of marriage. Maybe it sounds a little boring compared to the honeymooning stage. The lovers releasing their bottled-up emotions. Usually unexpressive males manage to whisper sweet nothings. I read somewhere that the origin of that expression "sweet nothings" translated means "promises."

One Valentine's Day—the youngest were in their teens, the older ones had left the nest—some daring child discovered Chief's love letters to me. When they set the table, they had a letter at every plate except Chief's and mine. They called us to dinner, announcing the rules of the occasion. (I did not know they were going to do this. And I don't know to this day which child dreamed it up.) I strongly suspect it was the MC for the evening. The MC said in place of our regular handholding Moravian blessing, each child would read a letter.

It didn't take Chief and I long to figure out they were our love letters.

Such promises you wouldn't believe. They got their biggest kick out of Chief's comment, "I didn't promise all that, did I?"

The older set found out about it. They couldn't believe the younger ones had such nerve. Or that we shared such a good laugh. They all came over to read the love letters. They couldn't believe the strict disciplinarian, Chief, could write such mushy stuff. They announced they were witnesses and he'd better get on with his promises. They agreed there are two ways of achieving success: by putting your shoulder to the wheel or putting your head on the shoulder of the man at the wheel. They said that I was a success—I had married a promising man.

These years may sound staid, but I can assure you they're not. It's not a case of passion dwindling into affectionate patting. This is love. Steady love. This is still the love-and-liking period. Times you love more than you like your mate. Times you like more than you love your mate. But as much as Chief exasperates me, as much as I can't stand him one fourth of the time, I love him more than anything in the world. I couldn't live without him. That's true after over four decades.

Role changing is fun. From lover to beloved. From beloved to lover. Rule changing is fun. New rules and old rules. Some we discard. Outgrow. Some are fast.

Few couples forget the serious rule they developed in their honeymooning stage. We cannot accept any invitation for us as a couple until we check with the other spouse. No matter how appealing or who's assumed the power play for the day. Who's in charge? Who hasn't gotten or shared a laugh when someone calls and asks for the boss? That is confusing when there's a partnership. It's embarrassing to others. Some parents are like the oldie story of the Martian who says, "Take me to your leader." In most households, it's the Little Leaguer.

You wonder where some couples get their marriage rules. From the television talk shows? The psychiatrist's couch? Or a political poll? You'll never find the answers to God's Plan for the Family in a psychology textbook. No. It's in the Book—the Bible. It's all there for those willing to read the book—1 Peter 3:7 for starters.

This "who's in charge" is settled once and for all. But it doesn't give a man an excuse to lord it over his wife and family. Ephesians tells us this truth. When the husband really loves his wife as much as he loves himself, is willing to give his life for her, there's no room for "lording it over." There is none.

The Bible puts to rest modern-day confusion. Answers as well as questions about marriage are all in there waiting for any and everyone to read. A lot of folks don't read the Bible because we're afraid of the answers.

Chief and I agree on the important things. Like other couples, it's the daily little things that we have to iron out. That's why a set of rules of behavior, spoken or written, makes sense. Defines a reasonable guideline. It helps us both to halfway know what the other is going to do in certain circumstances.

Rules should be products of mutual agreement. This diffuses many timebombs of potential arguments. It's based on "we," not "me." If I catch Chief on a rule violation, he knows I'm not just in a bad mood. But that we'd *both* agreed to the rule in an earlier, more rational, calmer moment. Jesus came to tell us the rules were not as important as the *spirit* of the rules. So keep that in mind.

Not all these rules protect us from each other. Some protect our public image. For instance, both of us abhor arguing in front of others about anything. Our relationship. Our children. Our differences of opinion. We've frowned on this behavior so long, neither of us has to give it a second thought. Never a fear of being attacked. We could argue about working mothers, church hierarchy, or the snatching of Dixie. But, God save the other if one of us says, "Oh, _____'s still seeking *your* approval." This may seem overly cautious. We all have sensitive spots.

Like kids playing a game, we remember the rules if we play enough. Our rules can cover anything from, The last one out of bed, make it (although it's more fun and easier, if we *both* do), to "Off comes the head of the one that leaves a tad of milk in his glass." Especially if it's left on some almost hidden end table.

We no longer have to discuss who takes out the garbage. It's the one who doesn't cook. No need to discuss. It's a rule. We came into the vacation rule years ago. We don't have to do what the other one wants. We're free. If I long for the beach, it's okay. As long as he doesn't have to go. Granted most wives are very good about vacations, according to their husbands. One told me that each year she said, "I'll go anywhere you like. Then she hands me a list of places I'd like!"

I convinced Chief years ago he's crazy to spend his free time paying for a vacation he hates because someone else thinks he "should." He agreed. I've enjoyed taking the kids to the beach. More times than not, he's joined us on the weekends. During his midlife crazies, the children thought a vacation was a relief without Chief. I'd point out to them how lucky they were to have a father that was a good provider. A father that saw to it they went to the beach even though *he* couldn't. He was allergic to the sun.

Now that my kids are grown and gone, I still enjoy the shore. Chief enjoys his home golf course. If you love each other, you want to see the other one happy. Surely does run up the phone bills, but it's a small price to pay for contentment.

People who think television has destroyed conversation probably don't pay the phone bill. I have to call Chief, or he, me, almost nightly while apart. That's a mutual-agreement pact. A desire. I have been known to take his worn tee shirt with me to drape over my pillow. Makes for better sleeping.

I have been known to lug my pillow into motels in a purple-and-white-dotted pillowcase. Only one doorman commented, "Man, those are some big dots on that pillowcase." I laughed. I was ready, "Linus has his blanket." We both laughed.

To get the hang of marriage is to be willing to work at it. Most of us think a little more experience will do the job. Then after several decades of marriage, we realize experience is what we imagine we have until we get more.

It's a you-ain't-seen-nothing-yet feeling. So hang in there. There *is* life after children. Especially after they've grown and gone.

13

Grown and Gone and Back Again:
You Can't Get Away
from Your Mother

Chief and I made many discoveries. The nine were grown and gone. We delighted in knowing we could still have a good time together. We thought we'd miss the "good old days" when Bedlam was bouncing. They were called "the good old days" because the days were old and worn out but we weren't. We were determined to enjoy ourselves every day, right now. If we don't, what'll we be nostalgic about in the year 2000?

I've seen so many couples mope around the empty house when the children are gone. Maybe we would have. But before we could count the missing buttons on the sofa cushion, the children were grown, gone, and back again.

Sometimes it's to check on us, to see how we could possibly make it without them. Each has a different concern. One is afraid we'll quit having those crazy fun parties we had when they were buzzing around. I do like to entertain, but when the kids left, so did my help. It was no fun making the "welcome" signs by myself. It was no fun dreaming up new themes or place cards.

About the only entertaining I did was Chief's dental-study club. It was a pleasure to cook for them. They all like to eat. They put up with anything I expose them to. Sometimes it's a German meal, Mexican, or Chinese with appropriate tags on the food. Men like to know what they're eating. Once I tired of trying to have pretty parties. I used the checked tableclothes, found an old limb in the backyard. Filled a bandana handkerchief with fake fruit. Tied the bandana to the stick, like a hobo would sling over his shoulder. The hobo doll was standing in a pile of fake money. He wore a sign that said, "I made mine in dentistry."

The before-dinner snacks were sardines (in the can), huge dill pickles, and old-fashioned soda crackers. I really had to search for those big crackers. I found an old country store outside of town that still carried them.

My standard dessert was homemade ice cream. Now that was fun when all nine were home. This is a two-gallon hand-turned job. Chief had to get a couple of the grown-and-gones back again. I was so disoriented in my kitchen without my usual built-in help, I forgot to have any chocolate syrup on hand. They always saw to it we had their favorite topping. I'm a purist. At the last minute I had one of my "great ideas." I'd make some. I had no recipe. I found a box of cocoa with a fudge recipe on it. I figured if I followed that and did not cook it the usual length of time, it would have to turn out to be chocolate sauce.

Dream on. It looked great. The men were delighted with the change of pace in their meal. The peanuts in the shells were fun. Hadn't had a sardine in years and all that. The corned beef and cabbage they gobbled up, along with fresh cornbread. But when the ice cream appeared, there were sighs of delight.

These signs of delight soon erupted into bellylaughs. The first unsuspecting guest heaped my homemade chocolate syrup all over his ice cream. It set up like concrete. Just as fast. Just as dangerous. His mouth was full. This dentist's teeth were trapped in chocolate. So thick he couldn't get his teeth apart to speak. Tears filled his eyes. Tears filled the eyes of the onlookers. He not only didn't think it was very funny, he was about to hit the panic button.

Luckily I had made a big pot of coffee. I rushed a hot cup to him pronto. After much swilling and sipping and general discomfort, he was able to part his teeth and speak: "Man, what happened, Libbylove?"

I was too concerned to be embarrassed.

"Oh, I'm so sorry," I hugged him. "I tried out an experiment. It didn't work!"

The rest of the gang thought that was the best party they'd been to in a long time. At least I make their wives look good.

As you know, my idea of a clean room is to sweep it with a glance. So once I get cleaned up, I do my entertaining. Chief declared that for three weeks at the time the bedspread in our room would be coats. And you do know, don't you, what the most dangerous time in any American household is? Thirty-five minutes before company is supposed to arrive. If you're a husband, suddenly the whole house is off limits. Chief always said a husband is a person who is under the impression he bosses the house, when in reality he only houses the boss.

One of the things Chief and I discovered in the grown-and-gone stage was that we made the messes. We had made them clean up theirs. We discovered we could keep a phone warm, too. We discovered quiet. We rediscovered communication. We discovered there *is* life after children, even nine.

Between my projects and Chief's projects, there's hardly a bit of tabletops showing. If it's not income tax he's working on, it's retirement plans. My writing nest is only inviting to rats. (And you know how I feel about rats. I agree with Erma Bombeck. Rats shouldn't have all the fun. They're plied with the food and drinks that are bad for us.) We've got the only rug in town with a six-inch pile—of newspapers.

This direct dialing has added a brand-new ailment to my repertoire: cauliflower forefinger. I admit I want to call our children every Sunday night. I don't, but I want to. It's leftover from the on-the-road-again college days. I slept better knowing they arrived safely.

Sometimes I'm lucky and they call me. It's only natural I talk to the out-of-towners more than those in town. Those in town take for granted I'm okay, or that Chief's happy on the golf course, or busy working. But the out-of-towners are different. They hadn't left Bedlam very long before I started getting calls.

"Mom, call me. I'm always calling you. Just because I'm way down here doesn't mean I'm not your baby anymore. You know I want to know what's going on at home. You told me I'd always be one of your babies! Call me!"

Chief says, "Libbylove, I don't mind your calling our out-of-towners. But just give them the short version."

"How are you?"

"Fine. And you?"

"Fine, thank you."

"Good. I love you."

"I love you, too. Thanks for calling."

Chief says, "That might not mean much to you—but to the telephone company it's worth eight-billion dollars on long-distance calls."

When the nine come back again, sometimes it's to borrow a big pot or serving dish to use when they're entertaining. If a son, maybe it's to talk to Chief, usually about financing. In fact he has a new name, Daddy Loan. When the last one left for college, he left an emptiness behind him. It was our savings account. But Chief's so good about staking them in business or a home, the telephone is always for him. There's not much call for mothering. We do talk over immediate concerns. We enjoy each other's company when we get to see each other. But they're grown, gone, married, and parents. So to prepare for this stage, I took writing lessons.

For seven years I took creative-writing lessons. I signed us up, hoping to interest a friend of mine who was suffering from the empty-nest mess. She was an avid reader. A great conversationalist. Has all the makings of a good writer. We had an outstanding professor from our local university.

The first night about fifty showed up for class. The next week only twenty-five. How do you account for that? Easy. That first night, when we sat down, he gave us pencil and paper and said, "Write!" You've never seen such a shocked class. Write? What about? It never occurred to them they'd have to write. The assignment was to write about what we had to go through with to get to class. I had that made, hands down. I was just writing away. Time flew.

Next week only half the class came back. That included my friend. I was hooked. What an addiction. There are times I loath it. Most of the time I adore it. It's like having a tiger by the tail, you can't let it go. You never know if it's going to eat you one piece at the time or consume you in one fell swoop.

It took me seven years to learn how to write an incomplete sentence. I had a professor that would take his finger and point out, word for word, the ones I should leave out. He said, "We think in phrases, we speak in phrases, we should write in phrases." So. I'm hard put to write long sentences. I do, strictly, to please whatever editor I'm working with. To his taste. I do a weekly newspaper column that I enjoy. You'd have to love writing to write. It's hard, often lonely, work. But if you're gonna write, you're gonna write.

I think writing is one of the best life-after-children activities. That doesn't mean to write to be published, necessarily. But to record your life. No one else has lived it. No one else has had the same experiences. You could leave such a gift to your loved ones.

Speaking is something else I enjoy. I was one of five Mothers-of-the-Year in our county. I was asked to tell about some of my experiences raising nine. One of the talks I give is "There Is Life After Children." So hang in there. I come to prove it.

It is really a it's-never-too-late-to-do-what-you-want-to-do talk. When the nine were leaving home, they'd say, "Libbylove, you've just got to do your thing." I'd explain to them I hadn't done my thing in so long, I didn't know what it was. But I would try.

I found time to look in the mirror. I remembered that solemn vow Chief and I took that we'd grow old together. From my reflection, it looked like I was going ahead without him. So I got on a regular exercise kick. I didn't jog. I never liked the pained looks on their faces. With nine kids I didn't want to get into any more pain. So I tried walking. It wasn't easy. I was afraid I'd get run over by the joggers. We have so many in our neighborhood, even the dogs are hoarse.

Chief got into the act. He told all his friends now that our nine were grown and gone, he was going to do something drastic. Years ago he put me on a pedestal. Now he put me on a diet. Of course diets don't work unless you do. I found the hardest part was making up my mind I wanted to get some weight off. Fortunately, I'm stubborn. When I make up my mind, you couldn't tempt me at all. Food I shouldn't have doesn't even look tempting. Crazy, isn't it?

When I'm out of control, I'll eat absolutely anything that doesn't eat me. Doesn't have to be tasty, pretty, or nutritious. Just available. My papa was like that. Could look at food and get fat. I saw him do more than look at it. Food was always important in the hotel I grew up in. If the food wasn't good, no one would come.

My mama was "in control" at all times. She came from the perfect-posture era. They worked at it. Her pet thing was to walk by and tap me lightly between the shoulder blades. I knew that meant to straighten up. She had the best habits. Changing my habits has been a lifelong struggle.

The importance of establishing and maintaining good habits was drilled into me daily while growing up.

"Libbylove," she'd say, "A good habit frees the mind from having to consider routine things. Mundane details. Enabling us to concentrate on more demanding tasks. Oh, there are benefits alright. The mind can then devote its entire attention to unfamiliar stimuli. Thus more challenging."

This childhood training was irksome to me, but a Godsend when I was raising my nine. If I hadn't had those good health habits ingrained, I'd be in much worse shape today—mentally, spiritually, as well as physically. Mom was quick to remind me that habits have to be practiced like our backhand in tennis, like picking up after ourselves, or refusing an extra cookie. The same is true of "Good morning," "Great meal," or "I love you."

The implications of forming good habits are tremendous. I surely tried to teach mine. I described how in *The Pains and Pleasures of Parenthood*. How we learn, how we remember, even how we perceive our masculinity and femininity are all matters of habit.

We can bring a bunch of bad habits into marriage that cause more misery than mirth. Me? I still think the best way to break a habit is to drop it. It's hard to discard our bad habit crutches, get rid of our dependence. Have you ever tried to unlock a baby's hand from around your finger? Prying—but trying not to hurt the little one? Getting rid of a habit is just that difficult, no matter how undesirable, even dangerous our bad habit could become.

We all have good intentions. When the grown-and-gone-and-back-again gather, we discuss progress or backsliding in our habits. We all have great intentions. Make resolutions. Try to sift through our habits. Deciding which ones to keep. Which ones to give up.

There are so many conflicting reports about what's "good or bad" for us. If we'd read and reread the Bible, it would make life simpler as well as happier. Making resolutions are said to be like broiled lobster. You have to pick through an awful lot to find any meat.

The wife of the great comic-strip philosopher was listening to him pontificate about bowl games. He was bemoaning the fact not everyone comes out a winner. He said, "Life is just a big bowl game. Some people win. Some people lose." His wife retorted, "The least you could do is play."

The big baddies, the sinful habits, are those that keep us out of the Eternal Kingdom. They call for change (see 1 Cor. 6:9-10). We can change. God made us of "matter" so we could. Gave us choices. With God's help, we ingrain the right ways in our minds. The Master Motivator has the Map. It's called developing character.

- No one can master a habit who doesn't want to. Can't do it alone.
- Stop the sinful habit immediately. Cold Turkey.
- When we've broken our habit, be willing to help those with the same habit.

Changing from a negative harmful way of life to a happy productive outgoing person takes God's help. Rest assured He will help. He wants his children happy, healthy, safe, and productive.

Chief and I have nine happy, healthy, productive children, Thanks be to God. When our grown-and-gone come back again, checking on each other's habits is a natural thing to do. We care about each other. Monitoring one another's habits is one way to show it. "You're getting an extra handle there"; or "Is that a gray hair I see? Don't tell me you're going to take after Mom's side." They spend a lot of time deciding or denying whose side of the family they take after. I find it amusing at all times. Sometimes hilarious. After all that trying to tell them how each of us is unique, they insist, ". . . but you're just like Edward." Or "Aunt Jane." Worse yet, "You're just like Libbylove. Always fussing over somebody."

Today's youth, mine included, view; "Can I get you anything?" as subservient. Not an expression of "I love you," which it surely is. When you love someone, you not only want the best for them, you want to do things *for* them as well as *with* them. It's a pleasure.

Now, grown-gone-and-back-agains are raising us. I've learned when they say, "May I get you a cup of tea?" or "Let me take that bag for you"—to mimic their tone of voice and say—"I can do it myself, thank you."

We exchange glances, then laughs. They've learned. Don't deprive someone of the pleasure, satisfaction, and opportunity of doing something nice for someone else.

It delights me to see our grown-gone-and-back-agains come check on us. Thanks be to God, they're swinging into fulfillment-oriented goal setting. Not strictly achievement-oriented goal setting. They're really getting the hang of it. Button-popping delights, they're still more pleasures than pains of parenthood.

Chief says I should work up another talk called, "Children Forever."

They are grown and gone and back again. I know I was one of those. I never outgrew the need for my mom's advice. My papa died three weeks after our hotel burned, from smoke inhalation, on my twelfth birthday. So my mama was my rock. I not only had her good advice, I had lots of love and support.

We never can get away from our raising. Some try very hard. But you can't. Temporarily you might stray. But those genes, those hours spent bending the twig, those precious moments with newborns, pay off. You can, as a mother, never give too much. Things, yes. Time and attention, no. Give it all you've got. Then learn to back off. Cut the apron strings. Then, if they come home again, that's the icing on the cake. The reward. You gave them all you had. You owe them nothing more.

You just hope and pray they read, marked, learned, inwardly digested, and remembered to show they abide by the commandment, "Honor Thy Father and Thy Mother." That they do this out of respect and love, not just tradition.

A tradition is something you have when you can't think of something new. I've always suspected traditions. If they're done out of duty, not love, they are meaningless. I've seen folks, through the years, get in a peck of trouble that way. I'm not talking about family traditions, but friends. Particularly if it involves Christmas, even New Year's. Anything you do year after year, you should think twice about. That routine soon becomes a tradition. I've seen friends outgrow each other in many ways. But they're locked into situations that can pinch. Particularly if, for any reason, it's hard to remain friends. Younger marrieds are prone to fall into these traps. Think twice before accepting.

When we have a family gathering, it can be traumatic. We're talking thirty-two. It's especially a culture shock to those marrying into this outfit. If they brought their beloved to Bedlam before marriage, that made it easier. A mob of verbal, expressive, outgoing people isn't comfortable for everyone. The teasing, the pushing-and-shoving matches males sometimes get into worry pacifist females. When they were small, the boys delighted the different ways sparring or wrestling was described. One family called it "horsing around." We called it "wild goating." Whatever you call it, the activity's the same.

When they first were grown and gone, they'd come back again for some basketball games. Even after they were married, their wives said they often looked lost. I reckon they wondered, "Where did everybody go?" They were used to people around. Usually, their spouse would say, "Oh, go ahead and call your brothers for a game."

If the weather was bad, they'd come for pool games in Bedlam's basement. We had a pool-and-Ping-Pong table. They enjoyed coming back to it on occasions. The occasions got less and less, as expected, with the years and with the arrival of grandchildren—our reward.

When they do come back on those rare times—like Christmas, Thanksgiving, special church activities—and their spouses say they revert right back to their childhood behavior. You would think it's a Tall-Tales Contest. All the wornout stories they love to tell about big family life. Number-three son entertains his own son, describing the bedroom at Trinity Treat where he slept. It had two bunk beds and a single bed in the huge room. If the child's eyes aren't popping out by then, he tells him how he hated to get off the school bus in the afternoon for fear he had another baby brother.

Number-two son says, "Togetherness to me is my wife leaning over me (while I'm watching the Atlanta Hawks basketball team) asking,

'What inning is it, dear?' I tell her it's the 7th. Give her the score. She goes back to her reading, content in the knowledge that she's making this marriage work."

So the stories go. Females who join the family have to like sports or else. Luckily, they do. If not, they're doing a super job to make their marriages work. Looks like they've made up their minds to be happy and are.

Communication is the biggest problem in big family life. I've threatened to get out a newsletter. I'd like to think we can communicate with one another better than a lot of families just because there're so many opportunities. That's not necessarily so. No amount of communication will produce a smooth-running, disagreement-free family. As much as we long to be understood by our family or understand our family, we should not expect it. Yet we do. And we should work at it.

Studying each other is a lifelong interest. We all change. Yet some of my children think a brother or sister is a certain way forever—as if set in concrete. We all change. That's even more reason to try to understand and be understood.

If any member of the family is guilty of being preoccupied primarily with self, he or she is miserable. Always wanting to be understood by the other brothers and sisters. Some even get out the pitypot once in a while. Or have spells of withdrawal. They don't come right out and say so, but infer that they don't want to be with their family.

The magic of the multiplication table works in a large family. There could be a cause for concern if all thirty-two birthdays had to be celebrated one at the time. Sometimes I've been known to have January birthdays in July. But then I might just take the honoree out alone. I've never figured out the way *they* like best. Since I'm outnumbered, I pull a Frank Sinatra. I do it "my way."

After all, Christmas, Easter, Thanksgiving, weddings and other family gatherings bring out the troops often enough for them. These events draw a crowd. Now we *do* have to hire a hall.

The more these gatherings force the grown-and-gones to be together as adults, it warms my heart. I see their views change. They begin to appreciate each other. They are more preoccupied with understanding the other. What a difference. I think they're beginning to realize you're only young once—but you can be immature indefinitely.

Have you noticed as soon as we feel understood, we put our knives down long enough to make ourselves better understood. As Lincoln said, "We're about as happy as we make up our minds to be."

These are the fun times. Chief and I enjoy our grown-and-gones when they come back again. Bedlam's still open. The Complaint Department's not as busy as it once was, but it's still open. I'm still the family "shock absorber." Still have my Meanest-Mama big ears ready to listen— whether it's happy reports like winning an election or a trip somewhere. It could be a raise or the birth of a baby. I'm happy for and with them.

When it's bad reports—financial reverses, disappointments, the death of a friend—I'm sad with them. When the youngest son's wife left him, I grieved just as much as he did. I not only was a shock absorber, but a rock. His faith was tested. It was rough. But he kept his faith and the belief that God had something better in store for both of them. He learned to be thankful, grateful that she was honest with him. Better now than later. Especially when there might be children involved. They parted friends.

As there is life after children, he learned there is life after divorce. So he's kept smiling, kept the faith, and knows he can count on The Dear Lord. He knows he can count on Chief and me. That's what family's all about. In the good times and bad. Checkout time's eighteen at Bedlam. But they're always welcomed back.

14

In-laws or Outlaws?
You Can Pick Your Friends

Mothers-in-law are a lot like seeds. You don't really need them, but they come with the tomato. You can pick your tomato, but not your mother-in-law.

It only takes one wedding ceremony to make you a mother-in-law.

You can pick your friends but not your relatives or your in-laws.

I'm a mother-in-law to seven. To date, I have fourteen in-laws. Win a few, lose a few. The numerical bit is complex. Its joy is simple. I like variety and I have variety. Each one is unique. Thanks to World War II, I have in-laws of Greek, German, and Italian descent. The rest are Anglo-Saxon Protestants. Their uniqueness adds spice to our life. Sometimes people will say to me, "I don't know all your children." I usually reply, "I have so many you're bound to find *one* you like." I love them *all.*

The same goes for my in-laws. I have so many, you're bound to find *one* you like. I love them *all.* Although marriage is nature's way of keeping people from fighting with strangers.

Luckily, most of my in-laws live nearby. So I've come to know them as they really are—special people. The relationship of in-laws to Chief and I, and each of the fourteen to each other could be mind boggling. It is more complicated due to the sheer numbers involved. From my standpoint, it's more demanding because Chief and I have sixteen grandchildren plus fourteen in-laws. The more to love. The less time to share.

Everyone has their own particular quirks. Quirks can be pleasant or unpleasant, amusing or irritating. Our "international" in-laws have distinctive traits of behavior. besides their speech. Most have lived in the

South since they were brides. Their eccentricities make them more fun. Our Anglo-Saxon-Protestant in-laws have their uniqueness. Chief and I have our fair share.

Some Southerners enjoy and encourage individuality. We hug our family's oddities, idiosyncracies to our bosom. We spend hours telling tall tales about our relatives. In some parts of our country, even if they know their relatives, they wouldn't dare talk about how "different" they are. They're locked in closets or whispered about behind backs. We enjoy regaling captive audiences with stories of the peculiarity of Aunt Jane or Cousin Billy.

Aunt Jane smoked cigars. That was an improvement. Aunt Polly, Jane's aunt, dipped snuff. Either were ready with retorts, flashes of wit, "If at *my* age, you've done (this and that) I've done, then *you* can talk about me." None of us could match their courage, fortitude. So nobody dared to cast the first stone. In spite of their unexpected actions or habits that differed from what our generation would consider normal, we loved and respected them.

I come from a long line of strongly independent personalities. We weren't expected to think, look, or act alike. The only thing we had in common was our love of God. When you get a long line of folks with "God's on my side," you're up against something.

You didn't dare talk about Uncle Harvey. He refused to wear any ties but bow ties. You admired his incredible energy. A man of the cloth, he could put on a beautiful church service all by himself. He'd say his words, reading the Bible and preaching the sermon. And then he would plop down at the organ and belt out, "Faith of our Fathers," singing out more lustily than anyone in the little church.

There are some young folks today that still enjoy hearing about the "olden' days." Storytelling is coming back. I was comparing my strange assortment of relatives with a college age friend awhile back. He was telling me about his ancestor who sold Lydia Pinkham. I told him one of my grandfathers found a mail-order bride after my grandmother died. We compared notes about family duels and feuds. His stories were matched, one by one, with mine.

Aha! I thought of one.

"One of my grandfathers was an Abolitionist!"

That didn't faze him.

"One of mine fought for the *king!*"

There are rules, unwritten but respected. You only talk about *your* relatives. You only tell jokes on yourself or your mate, with permission. Right behind "love of God, integrity" and all those good traits, a family with a good sense of humor comes in second. Good humor doesn't make our personal or family problems go away. But it does ease us over some tight spots.

Americans are grateful, truly blessed. Unlike those countries behind the Iron Curtain and the Bamboo Curtain we are able to enjoy a good laugh together.

In getting acquainted with our new in-laws, some folks have real problems. So many jokes and put-downs have been written, it creates a mental and emotional fence that's unnecessary.

Most of the time you're lucky enough to meet your prospective in-laws before the wedding festivities. It does make things so much easier to enjoy that super-exciting "wedding day." Too often, you're meeting them for the first time and suddenly a fog of self-consciousness rolls over you. You can't think of anything to say. Or if you think of something, it seems completely stupid, or downright dull.

You become conscious that you are overdressed—or underdressed. You're either too fat or too thin. You've suddenly acquired four right hands and six left feet, worse yet, no head at all. Your mind just shut down.

You look around at other people—so poised, well-adjusted, getting along just great. Being around verbal people intimidates you even more. You want to run away. But your legs are like putty. You couldn't run if you had to. You're glued to your seat.

You remember your friend's teasing you about becoming a mother-in-law. You remember the jokes:

"Did you know we now have a law that prohibits outside agitators from crossing state lines. I sent a copy of it to my mother-in-law."

"Until I met my mother-in-law, I didn't realize there was a Mrs. Scrooge!"

You have vowed *not* to be an agitator, *not* to be Mrs. Scrooge. But you don't want your new in-laws to think you're a deaf mute, either, although the father-in-law would probably love it.

Don't despair, in my cullings I came across secrets I want to share. Some I've gathered, like a bunch of sesame seeds, from talking to the most popular and well-adjusted people I know, from living so long—thanks be to God—from interviewing for the newspaper, and from reading and collecting clippings on "getting acquainted."

Some folks are such extroverts, they don't know why they're not afraid or embarrassed when newcomers appear. Others have fought "shyness" all their lives. Some have been through various degrees of self-consciousness. Their answers, that solved things for them, might help us all unlock the doors of our own self-consciousness. Make people notice us. Be interested in us. And make them want to see us *again*. Just three short sentences "open sesame." They're like magic.

1. "You're different."
2. "You're wonderful."
3. "Tell me more."

Just because these sentences are magical, they are made of glamour, reek of romance. They should be handled with kid gloves. Dynamite can be just as dangerous. Like a lot of other things, use them incorrectly, you've spoiled their magical powers. Worse yet, you could bring laughter right down on your head. If you neglect to follow them up, they wither and die.

Practice using them correctly and I think we have stumbled upon the secret of charm and popularity. It just might give you courage to meet new people. Strangers will truly be people you haven't met. You'll never feel burdened with extra arms and legs, or feel helpless, embarrassed, and alone, wishing you were home!

I dare you, the next time you meet a new person, try one, or two—or if you're really brave—all three magic sentences. Then when you meet your new in-laws, or anyone else at the wedding festivities, you can hold your own with the best and rest of them.

There are rules. If followed, I believe the results will astound you. But like any magic, you've got to understand it to use it properly. You don't have to take my word for it. Just try it and you'll see results.

The number-one rule: you must be sincere. It's what's behind these sentences that make them potent—or useless. The word is *sincerity*.

1. "You're different." Common sense says you can use this on almost every new person you meet. Why? You wouldn't be interested in attracting just one of the herd. God made each of us different. So, go to it:

"You're different." "You're not like everybody else I've known." "There's something about you that's different."

You hit a nerve. This person thinks he's different. We all do. Maybe he's been aware of it for years. Maybe others have told him (using your magic). Maybe they haven't and he really needs to know it.

"What makes you think so?" "How am I different?" "Whadda' ya' mean?"

Then it's up to you. You can surely find something different. Look at them as an interesting, different person. (But if you aren't interested in people, you might as well stop right here. God made so many people. If you're not interested, your life is doomed to drabness, dullness, and some cases, being almost worthless.)

I'm assuming you're really a nice, warm, human being—just a little uncomfortable meeting new people, especially new in-laws-to-be. Ask the magic question. The answer will unlock the floodgates of your mind. You'll know *why* that person's unique, interesting. And you'll say so, maybe not in many sentences, just a provocative sentence or two. And watch!

He'll ask you how you knew so much about him. And you reply, in just one or two short remarks. Before long he's telling you that *you're* different. Maybe you've moved on along to something else just as pleasant and entertaining.

You're on your own now. It's up to you to follow through.

2. "You're wonderful" must be used with the greatest care. It's the most powerful of these sentences.

If you're meeting your new in-laws-to-be, that might be coming on too strong for the occasion. However, "You're great," "You're terrific," "You're something else," or any compliment you feel comfortable with will do.

Even with "You're great," you must be able to follow it up. Don't say it if you're not sincere, or if you cannot *show* why you think so.

"Jim says you have been some kind of great father." Other examples:

It may be because of a book he's written, a song he sang at the wedding rehearsal, the way he managed to get you a glass of punch in the crowd—anything. Look for things to praise and compliment people. You'll find them. But it must be because of something real. You'll have to say what it is, unless you're using it as a "thank you." It works for that, too. Then you really don't need to follow up.

If you're "always a bridesmaid" type, or attending the wedding, and you want to attract the opposite sex, "You're wonderful" is the sentence to get you off to a good start. Any girl who has a whit of charm or personality at all can get along with just that. "You're wonderful," common sense again tells you, will have a greater effect if you're one-on-one with the opposite sex. You'll be surprised. The people you least expect will accept it. Some fall for it and rightly so, *if* it's sincere and used correctly.

3. "Tell me more." It's last because it's obviously better as a follow-up. Sometimes you might choose to use it as your first sentence. But "Tell me more" can't be used until the *other* person says something. The other two sentences can start things.

"Tell me more" is better than just being a good listener. Good listening used to be the key. But too often the listener only listened. Listening's not enough. What we're trying to do is start something—at least a conversation. Listening not only doesn't start anything, it doesn't *add* anything to a conversation. It throws the other person into a monologue. A conversation involves two people—dialogue.

Listening still has its place, but that comes later on, *after* you've used your magic. Magic's first, when you most need it, to start a conversation. It eggs the other person on. You can say, "Please go on," "Won't you tell me the rest?" "I'm really so interested in that." Just "Tell me more" works wonders.

Look the person in the eye, as if you want to hear what *they* have to say more than you want to hear anything else in the world. Observe those people who are showered with attention. You'll soon see what it is, they concentrate on the person they're with.

The catch? Again, the word back of this magic of starting conversations—sincerity.

These three magic sentences can come in handy. Not just with meeting new in-laws. You may need them to help open not only the door to conversation, but to friendship. You want your new in-laws to be friends, not outlaws.

All the magic of these three sentences will be canceled unless you're not only sincere, but warm and really interested. If not, there's no way you can follow through. Insincerity cancels the magic.

The new in-laws, like yourself, want to be liked. They may have a shell, too. Or are embarrassed and ill at ease meeting new people just like you are. You know now, how to use magic to break down their defenses, to overcome their embarrassment. Just as you've learned to overcome yours. Smooth phrases are fine, momentarily, but most everyone feels and resents insincerity.

Send out that warmth, affection, and sense of humor, and it will come back to you. I'm sure these sentences will work for you just as magically as those who told me about them. You've still got to give, to get. (You've seen where they've gotten me.)

Getting along with in-laws, or anyone for that matter, is not a matter of techniques, but a thing of the spirit. As America's best known psychologist, William James, said, "The human relations are the main thing." We know happy human relations are a spiritual achievement, another one of those gifts from God.

After the knot is tied, getting along with your own in-laws is a spiritual achievement. In some families, it's a miracle. You don't realize you're not only marrying your mate. You're marrying their family. This causes universal problems, according to Ruth Peale, "that no one escapes."

It makes it doubly hard, but doubly interesting since "somebody's daughter married somebody else's son." This makes understanding your in-laws so much better. Just put yourself in their shoes. You realize they have the same cares and concerns about the newlyweds as you do.

Scheduling is something else in our big family. Who goes to which mother-in-law's when? I refuse to get into that. In fact, I have wanted to spend holidays in different places just to avoid it. I'm all for tradition. But how can you meld tradition into a smooth situation when you have as many in-laws as I do? The children, now grown and gone, have different ideas of how they want to spend their holidays. Well they should. The married ones have their own traditions to set. I love them just as much if I don't get to spend a holiday with them. So I try to be flexible.

Those for whom "to grandmother's house we go" really means something I want to see them. I welcome them with open arms, especially if this is a tradition they want to leave to their own children. I honor and respect that, and love them for it.

For of my sets of in-laws live in town. How many turkey dinners can you eat in one day? Like most moms, I've been taken out, taken in, and taken for granted. Just so they get by for hugs and "I love yous," that is sufficient. The meal is great. But the sweet spirit is the important thing. I don't want anyone to come see me out of "duty," just love.

Three of my sets of in-laws live out of town. It's only fair the grown kids go see them. They don't get to see them as often. There are plenty of other times we can get together.

I know firsthand the resentments and problems families create themselves by insisting on having their way. If they don't get it, they get mad. Didn't we learn getting angry is a choice? Also when you get angry you are saying, "I want *my* way." A crust of bread shared with love is so much better than a feast served with resentment.

I've seen some mothers sigh and groan through the holidays and wonder why no one enjoys them. Others leave their husbands out of the planning altogether. It doesn't occur to include them. In our hotel, my papa was the spirit of Christmas. He loved getting it all going. Didn't mind paying for it, and had his ideas. Mama wasn't all that enthusiastic.

She was just her calm, in-control self. After all, the kitchen of our hotel was my mom's.

In lots of homes, the mother is Christmas all the way. The children aren't allowed to touch anything. I described my Christmases in *The Pains and Pleasures of Parenthood.* I never wanted mine to get caught up in the commercialization of Christmas. Never wanted them to forget Whose birthday we celebrate.

My attitude is often misunderstood, I'm sure. Of course I'd love, like every other grown-child to celebrate Christmas like we did in my hotel home. I miss gathering around the Christmas tree singing carols. Our rinky-dink plays. Music and drama were an important part of Christmas as well as going to the church services. But I married into a family that thinks that's silly. So I only had a few fun years of enjoying my own putting on plays and decorating the tree together. Nothing lasts forever, and that's just one of the stages that doesn't.

Presents? The greatest present mine can give me is to go to church with me. I don't think once a year is asking too much. They have their own churches, understandably, and own schedules. But I just can't tell you what it does for me to sit in the pew with them one more time. It doesn't have to be the whole mob. Although it would be nice once a year for fun. Not just funerals or weddings. However, one at a time is satisfying, fulfilling. Thanks be to God, I get the privilege and pleasure. That's why baby dedications are so special to me. Welcoming a newborn into God's family and our family, surrounded by the loving support of their parents, Godparents, thrills me.

Most of the mother-in-law jokes are poked at mothers who can't cut the apron strings. Fathers are less inclined to make a big deal of family relationships. They usually are so preoccupied with their jobs, they sometimes don't tune in to personal relationships.

In talking with others about their relationships with in-laws, I came to this conclusion—gender has nothing to do with anything. Some fathers are more sensitive, into personal relationships more than the mother. Some mothers are less inclined, believe it or not, to judge or criticize the person their child chose to marry.

In lots of instances, where one parent was deceased, the spouse looked to their in-law to be their surrogate mother or father. Certainly there is more love for in-laws than hits the press. We only hear about the "impossible" people. They're going to be impossible in any situation.

I was amazed Ruth Peale said she and her husband (Norman Vincent Peale) had a mutual agreement about their in-laws. They were very open with each other, and talked about their parents to each other. Although it might be rough at times, all faults were brought out, viewed, and laid on the line. She said it brought them "closer and make a greater depth of understanding between the two of them." They agreed to "say anything that came to mind" and found it the best form of ventilating.

"I do think we wanted each other to defend his parents. After all, a person who doesn't love his parents aren't likely to have much love capacity in him, for a married partner, or anyone else."

"I tell newlyweds, one of the greatest arts they have to learn, as a couple, is to talk together about each other's parents with absolute honesty and openness. Marriages can founder under impact of in-law problems."

My mama had a hands-off policy. I do, too, and I can see how it can be misunderstood. But I have seen some girls and men, too, completely dominated by their mothers. They either can't or don't make a decision without consulting their mother. Everything has to be reported and approved.

Assuming that what you think is good for you would be good for them is hardly kindness. Mother fixations are a reality. A man who always compares his wife with his mother and expects his wife to be just like her is fixated. Inferiority complexes and hypersensitivity can ruin even compatible marriages.

So to be good in-laws, we need to be good people first. If you really can't understand your mother-in-law, make a study of her. A calm, thorough, objective analysis of what makes her tick. Then we can begin to know what made her that way.

Chief's mother's father was killed when she was a tiny girl. She had to go live with her grandparents. She had brothers and sisters. Then when her mother remarried, she had a new set of brothers and sisters.

Together, her mother and new father had even more children. All of these things shaped her life, her values, her views.

This study of my mother-in-law made me understand her so much better. To understand her motives and actions. In the process, I learned an amazing amount about Chief. Why he's like he is. I realize his mother was the strongest influence before me. Trying to understand Chief's mother helped me understand him. I love Chief, therefore I love his mother. She made him what he is.

If sons-in-law remember to treat their wife's mother like a woman, not a piece of furniture, a bother, or an irritant, they'd be rewarded. In all relationships, we usually get back what we send. That includes in-laws, not just mothers-in-law.

I think our in-laws bring a new dimension to our family—more sparkle and love. They are a real blessing. They're like Chief and I—human beings, each with his or her own flaws and oddities, yet very lovable and supportive of our marrieds. They have that extra quality I appreciate—they're fun to be around.

One of the most fun times was Chief's Sixtieth Birthday Celebration. It was not only an opportunity for wishing Chief a happy sixtieth, it was a great chance to get together to celebrate "family." A sense of community with our children, grandchildren, friends and in-laws. A chance to see the Holy Spirit at work. Different ages, stages, backgrounds, and ethnic heritages coming together as one.

It's difficult for some people to comprehend Jesus' words, "For where two or three are gathered together in my name, there am I in the midst of them" (see Matt. 18:20, KJV.) When the Holy Spirit is in you and me, there is no getting away from it. It's not just in church, on Sunday. It's in your work place and play place.

You may not realize that the second oldest feast of the Church is not Christmas, but the Day of Pentecost. It comes fifty days after Easter. (Easter is the oldest feast day on the Christian calendar.) Pentecost celebrates the gift of the Holy Spirit.

The work of the Spirit, whether recognized or not, continues in every age, every individual, in every culture. It blends and binds people together, regardless of "where they came from" or where they're headed. The

Holy Spirit is not always obvious, or measurable. You look around at so-called Christians and wonder if they have a dab of it.

Once I was in a sharing group at my church. We were enjoying talking together about the wondrous things God had done in our lives for us and with us. A girl in her twenties was a guest. She told of an experience she had.

She had started to resent having no choice. Having to attend church services whether she wanted to or not. Away from home, at college, at last she could chuck the whole church bit.

She said she went out with some college friends one night to a coffee house. She thought it sounded like a swinging place, one she had heard about during the 60s. She noticed after awhile she saw no coffee, smelled no coffee, and wasn't offered any coffee. She said she looked around.

"These folks *looked* different. I saw no evidence of drugs or alcohol. Yet. Happiness, joyful, and fun-filled would describe them. No. I looked again. It was just like they had their headlights on."

"Then when they started singing, they were singing praises to the Lord. I looked at those headlights shining brightly. I didn't know what they had. But I *wanted* IT. I realized, 'Hey, they're Spirit-filled.' I could see the Holy Spirit in them. I could feel the Holy Spirit."

"I turned to the girl next to me and said, 'Are my headlights on?' Of course she didn't know at first what I was talking about. We have this battery, this great potential inside of us. All we have to do is turn it on. Let it shine. She assured me my headlights were on."

Then this young thing looked around the room at us and asked, "Are my headlights on?" Paused. "I hope so. Some days they're just on dim, or low. But. I don't ever want them not to be on. It just might light somebody's way." She looked us over, smiling, approvingly, "Yes, I see your headlights are on too. That's why we Christians have to get together, to check each other. To make sure we keep our headlights on."

Well, immediately I got out my pad and pen. I had heard words I had to keep. It would go right into my notebook of the unique ways people put words together. I just loved it. I've been checking my own headlights ever since.

The study of the Book of Acts is one of the most exciting things you can do—to read, learn, inwardly digest, and practice the Holy Spirit. That's one of the main ways we differ from our Jewish brothers and sisters. On the Jewish calendar, Pentecost was originally a feast day that fell fifty days after Passover. When Jesus became the New Passover, it was appropriate to continue Pentecost. It's a commemoration of that strange and wonderful event inspired by the Spirit (see Acts 2:1-4). The history of the event was well grounded in my faith. I was not totally aware of the impact until I studied *The Drumbeat of Love,* a study of Acts by Lloyd Ogilvie.

I knew the disciples went up into the upper room a defeated, defected, depressed bunch of men. Powerless. They came out totally transformed. They were filled with warmth, love, joy, energy. All because our Savior saved them. He filled them with the Holy Spirit. They were never the same.

Sure we know all that. The point we sometimes are apt to miss is: He embues us, too. I just thought it was priests, special holy ones. They received the gift. The gift of healing. All those many wonderful gifts, of blessing everyone they meet. I missed the whole point. He also brings the gift to us. I understood the "laying on of hands." It was a tremendous experience to have my pastor lay his hands on *my* head. That made a difference in my life. Yet, nothing had the impact on my personal walk in faith as the realization that we have the same powers, thanks be to God, through His Son, Jesus Christ. We can heal by touch. Energize another person. WE have those mighty powers as well as our seemingly small ones. Ministering day by day in our unique way to those around us. That blew my mind. Excited me no end.

Think of the recognition and cultivation of the Holy Spirit in our lives. It helps us in so many different ways to understand, to gain insight, to create, to love, to forgive, to hope, to plan and, most importantly, to *respond* to all that is given us.

If it could change those ragtag fishermen into spiritual giants who changed the course of history, think what it could do for us. Here and now. This Holy Spirit within us can inspire us to move out beyond the ordinary and the accepted. Energize us to try new things, to reach new heights and new depths. Most of all, to enable us to go on, when we feel our life is in pieces. When we are powerless. Yes, we are powerless without the Holy Spirit. This is the most wonderful of God's gifts to each of us.

Haven't you seen the Holy Spirit motivate and transform the most timid among us? It is beautiful to see. To see someone you know change from a fearful, tentative, dull, half-alive person, yet call themselves "Christian." They don't seem to know the meaning of "respond." You know the type—always talk of "dying." Not "living." Dying to sin. Dying to "worldly" interaction. The "Stop the World, I want to get off" type. Whining dependents, who have no life of their own. Their world gets smaller and smaller. A person wrapped up in himself is a small package. Worse yet, they pollute the environment with their negativism. Hide under the blanket of being "good." "Doing good." They do these things solely for the nagging need for others' approval.

"The size of a person's world is the size of his or her heart." Fully alive folks don't hide in the dark world of egocentricity, with a population of one. They are responders—filled with the Holy Spirit. Being a loving person is very different from being a so-called "do-gooder." Do-gooders actually sometimes use other people as opportunities for practicing their "acts of virtue," of which they keep careful count. Taking advantage of others to boost their own self-esteem.

People lovers learn to shift their attention to others, Away from themselves. People lovers care deeply about others. The difference between do-gooders and people lovers is the difference between a life that's an onstage performance and a life which is an act of love. Real love can't be imitated. You can see it. Feel it. You can't hide those blazing headlights when they're on bright.

Our sharing and caring must be genuine. If not, our love means nothing. One thing's certain, if we're going to make any progress in learning to live life more fully, we're going to have to learn how to love more—the hard-to-love as well as the easy-to-loves. The Holy Spirit is the Enabler.

Often the Holy Spirit motivates us. We've seen it motivate unlikely persons as well as the expected. The Holy Spirit inspired a neurotic, young genius to become Wolfgang Amadeus Mozart. God loved him, sent him the Holy Spirit to inspire, motivate, and enable him to compose beautiful music. God loves us, too. He is forever loving us. Think of the illustrious recipients of his unconditional love: Peter, the rock, wishy-washy, often caught in his own mouthtrap, even denied knowing the one who had loved him most; Martha, a Nervous Nellie, first-class worrier, whiner. Who can forget Saul of Tarsus, hellbent on eliminating Christianity from the face of the earth, until he made that bumpy trip to Damascus and found a loving Lord? In our own day, an old country woman proved it's never too late to develop your God-given talents. Grandma Moses became one of our most popular folk artists, an inspiration to us all.

Part of the full life includes a sense of community. A union of persons who share themselves. They try to understand their fellow human beings. They are *for* one another. They share themselves and their time in love. They have a sense of belonging to their families. To their church, and to the human family. They are full of the Holy Spirit. Their headlights are on. There is a place where their absence would be felt. They'd be really missed. Their deaths mourned. This is family. It includes our in-laws, grandchildren, children, friends.

This is what I work towards, pray for, in my own family—that we, as a family, with all the inclusiveness of that word—find the deep peace, contentment, and joy in belonging to the whole family of God.

Particularly in our daily coming togethers, constructive rather than destructive words and actions are exchanged. My prayer is for us to be filled with the Holy Spirit, who enables us to be flexible, not rigid in our attitudes. We create a climate and support line that enables our grandchildren to perform well, develop their talents in reasonable proportion. Learning to be adaptable and confident when change is thrust on them, or when they have those tough decisions that will change the course of their lives. Then they know we, the family, love them and God loves them—unconditionally. Spirit-filled, they keep their headlights on. It's a dark world out there. There's no better contribution we as parents can make than to produce good Christian children, full of a brisk energetic spirit and enthusiastic joy that comes from knowing our Savior.

In-laws or outlaws, we are one in The Spirit.

15

Real Relations:
What Else Becomes More
Precious
with Time? Friends

It is great to have friends when one is young, but indeed it is still more
so when you are getting old. When we are young, friends are, like everything else, a matter of course. In the old days we know what it means to
have them.
            —Edward Grieg

Edward Grieg (1848-1907) famous Norwegian composer, is best
known for his music But with all his fame, he never forgot to thank his
friends. This, from my packrat cullings, spoke to me. Friends are one
thing I can't do without. Like the Dear Lord, my Chief, and my family.

There are times when I'm so involved with my large tribe, I wonder
how in the world I could still have a friend. I can hardly cover all my
home bases, much less the outfield. They occupy "holy space." That
dimension of thoughts and prayers. They are always in my thoughts and
prayers.

To cope with the Empty-Nest Mess and The Midlife Crazies, I direct-
ed my drives into writing and speaking. No one has been more supportive
than my friends. Things haven't changed all that much, timewise. They
get the short straw still.

Any teeny-weeny honor I've received has been nothing more than a
reflection of the loving support of my family and friends. I try publicly
and in my daily contacts to give them credit. I wouldn't dream of
accepting an honor alone. I try to share any little recognition I've had
with all who were with me in its winning. A single credit becomes a debit.
If I should ever be the "crowning stone at the crest of the pyramid," I'm
very well aware it's the other stones which would keep me there.

My friends are always on my mind. Even if they don't know it. I was reading the newspaper about classes in "Friendship" being offered at a college. At least that's a step in the right direction. Some of the students I've observed seem to be majoring in "shrugging." The idea of "friendship" classes gave me an idea for one of my weekly newspaper columns. I want to share it with you. It's headline is, "Friendship Shouldn't Be Neglected":

"Friend is a loosely used word. It shouldn't be. A friend is a real treasure. Can you believe it's necessary for classes in 'Friendship' to be part of a college curriculum?"

Steve Saffron has fifty-six students in his friendship class at Scottsdale (Ariz.) Community College. He says the course is important because many people don't understand the value of friends, or the role they play in wellness. He said: "It's a neglected relationship in our culture."

I couldn't get this article off my mind. Have we gotten so busy we don't have time for friends? Are we becoming uncaring, unsharing?

Making friends was the first thing I tried to do when I moved, whether it was a new town, school, or job. Like many songs say, I can't get by without the help of my friends.

My friends haven't stood around and looked when I was in trouble, little or king-sized. They've gotten there on the double. One actually saved my life.

When things are going smoothly, my friends are always doing thoughtful things. When I seek much-needed advice, they take time to give it. When tempted, they won't let me sink. Besides, my friends are fun to be with.

Saffron says, "When I say friends, we're talking about choosing *quality* people." Doesn't that sound like mom? How many times have you heard yours say, "Birds of a feather flock together"? Remember the mini-sermons about the importance of the company you keep. "It'd better be good."

"We need a wide variety of friends if we're a growing, evolving person," Saffron notes. I couldn't agree more. I certainly learn something from everyone I meet. I've learned tidbits to profound truths from my buddies. Some are my Y-buddies I exercise with. I flop down on my knees to pray. They're my knee buddies. I bunch them according to common interests.

Saffron teaches, "A good friend, a close friend, you can't have too many because it takes too much energy. If you go through life and you have a few really good close friends, you've done okay. Finding those friends can be difficult." True. A good close friend is a treasure. Most of us can count those always-dependables on one hand. You might not see them for years. It matters not. You can take up where you left off with no explanations or apologies. Maybe you don't share common interests, just common values. Just love them the way they are.

We've always known we can't pick our relatives, but we can pick our friends. Saffron, who has been studying friendship for twenty years, says spouses or relatives are not fill-ins for other friends. "Even if we have that one juicy relationship, we'll still only have 50 percent of what we need. Life is very stressful, and friends are a way to promote health."

"One of the biggest mistakes people make when they get married or enter into a love relationship is dropping their friends," he says. "Then in later years, they realize they need friends."

According to Saffron, everybody senses the importance of friendship and feels that need, but people are afraid. He says, "They are afraid to take risks because they've been hurt or put down. I see the class as a place for them to implement what they do and try it out in a comfortable environment. The class is a safe place."

"We dance in the class, listen to music and readings. One of the things I've learned about maintaining friendships is humor and an open door to humor. What I teach in my friendship class is how to lighten up and play more," he said. "If you're going to maintain friendships you have to know how to have fun." Amen.

When the Man-From-Whom-All-Blessings-Flow dealt out treasures, friends were certainly among the dearest.

We've always know to "have a friend, be one." However, in this busy, busy world filled with people with the "hurry, hurry" disease, apparently somebody's not setting the good example of getting along. These things are supposedly taught at home. But, if nobody's home, what happens? Daddy's at work. Mama's at work. Children are in day care. Where are the teachers? The whole load is on the schoolteachers? What sort of shape are they in?

Somebody's observed that the trouble with the school system today is: the teachers are afraid of the principals, the principals are afraid of the superintendent, he is afraid of the school committee, they are afraid of the parents, the parents are afraid of the children, and the children are afraid of nobody.

If a visitor from Mars should examine our lifestyle he would be puzzled. If indeed he visited our schools and colleges, he'd ask, "Where are your books for teaching people how to get along with each other?" Chances are he wouldn't see a copy of the Bible there—the best Book in the world on getting along together. About the only way children today will learn would be in the "school of hard knocks."

Even very few college graduates have ever heard of any laws or rules for getting along with people. Yet the ability to get along with others is far more important for a successful life than all school studies combined.

In my packrat clippings, I found a tattered 1944 article I'd saved. In one of my many journals, I took down some notes I wanted to share with you:
These are two "ironclad laws of the mind for getting along with people" and "six ironclad rules for applying them" that are as "fixed as the laws that guide the stars." These techniques of winning people are the brainchild of Herbert Spencer, an English philosopher.

The first law is: "You dare not puncture the other fellow's ego." He talks about how cruel children can be to each other. Calling each other names. A boy with red hair is dubbed "Red." A fatty, "Tubby," even someone lame is dubbed, "Limpy."

The tragedy is that many adults never outgrow this. You're only young once. But you can be immature forever. The shy or bashful, skinny—name it—all get their egos bruised. All it does is lower the recipient's self-esteem. A sin. Research has shown that anything and "everything that frustrates the individual in preserving his ego produces aggressive conduct. Unless wisely guided, it will always be destructive conduct."

Until parents and teachers make it their business to train children, lead children, the direction they should go, what hope do we have for the future? I've written lots and given many talks on the importance of parenting, particularly mothering. Chief and I don't agree on the "working mothers" dilemma our country's in. I touched on this in an earlier chapter. I still think mothering is the most important job in the world. I just grieve for the children. Who's thinking of them?

Those first few years are so important. If every idea has been checked out, every avenue, to find a way to stay with your child. I do pray wherever they land that, for God's sake, it will be in a place where the "keepers" truly love children, where they won't lower any human being's self-esteem, especially that of a child.

I'd rather someone maim my child or grandchild physically than to lower its feeling of the security of its own ego. I tried, as I'm sure you've done, to guide my nine's self-esteem, nourish it, cherish it, understand it, teach it intelligent goals in life—but never lower it. There's plenty in the big, bad world trying to do that.

The second law for getting along with people is "The human mind may not be a machine, but it acts like one." In other words, human conduct is predictable. Spencer said if we have any doubts, all we have to do is "try calling the first man you meet a scholar and a gentleman, and the next one a liar and a scoundrel, and see where you land!" We know "A soft answer turneth away wrath."

Isn't it funny how everyone knows this biblical truth, yet fail to practice it. Half the troubles of the world are caused by neglecting to do this elementary thing.

Rule Number One: "You must be absolutely sincere." This rule you've seen running throughout these chapters. Sincerity is honesty. It is a beautiful thing and getting rarer and rarer in government, business, family life, marriage, and friendship. Often we're not honest or sincere with ourselves. How urgent is the call back to honesty? How important is it as Christians, in view of the recent religious strife, to present ourselves as friends of God? Not a frustration or irritation or embarrassment. I love this quote from an Episcopal bishop:

Our own friendship with God must be perceived by others as we present our Savior, or we may be seen as unauthorized judges of our fellowmen. The word "perceive" carries an element of shared meaning as something becomes appreciable or ponderable through another, especially through the senses. Let us be the aroma, the fragrance of Christ, to a fainting world.

Probably no one ever achieves absolute sincerity. Mainly because we have this innate tendency called "rationalization." This urge to give excuses for our conduct instead of reasons, in order to preserve our egos. I'm a past master at rationalization. I can make anything I do almost okay. I have to keep a constant check. I can fool myself like no other.

Rule Number Two: "You must make the other fellow believe in *you.*" No matter how sincere you may be, you must make the other fellow believe you are sincere. Usually your good reputation will precede you. Your good name, if you're living in your hometown. If you are in a strange place, you might play the game, "Who do you know?" You can strike a common note this way. Southerners often play "Who do you know?" So a good family name is a must. A must, too, is for you to uphold it. Guard it. The Bible speaks to the importance of a "good name."

Having letters of introduction is a help. So are quickly finding a church home and having a letter from your pastor. Join clubs you belonged to back home, wherever home was. Each person has to devise his own way of making the other fellow believe in you.

Rule Number Three: "You must believe in *other* people." The hardest people to get along with are suspicious people. Those who are always looking for hidden meanings in what you say or do. This type of warped personality frustrates you. The more you talk to them, the more they manage to twist what you say into meaning something else. You may think you've made your point, then they'll go back to something you innocently said previously. And say, "What did you mean by *that?*" You can tell 'em you meant just what you said. But they'll manage somehow to keep yakking about it for hours. A few clear statements would have settled it in five minutes, if they had ever learned to believe other people were just as honest and sincere as they.

Rule Number Four: "You must overestimate the other fellow's point of view." According to psychological studies, only about "four persons out of five would recognize themselves if they should meet themselves coming down the street. They do not even recognize their own hands. Or when they see their reflection in a mirror."

I can identify with that. I was walking into a hotel room, to pick up some couple we were going to dine with. I noticed as I passed a mirror on my left, some white-haired woman that looked vaguely familiar. I looked to the right and greeted my friends. Another couple were there also. On the way out of the room, I glanced into the mirror as it was facing me. The vaguely familiar white-haired woman was me!

The point—that we rarely recognize ourselves, our voice records, and so forth—in getting along with people is if we do not deliberately overestimate the other fellow's point of view, we are almost certain to overestimate our own. So if you really want to get along happily and effectively with your fellow humans, you must overestimate other peoples' personalities and points of view.

Rule Number Five: "Don't try to achieve superiority by making the other fellow feel inferior." You know the kind. The strong, silent male who never tells his wife or children he loves them. His wife and children beg for affection. It irritates him. He wants to know "What's the use of eternally telling you so?" According to psychologists, he is unconsciously trying to preserve his lord and master position by making his wife and children feel inferior. Others use the dominating, battle-axe system. To get their power kicks. Spencer said this kind of parent makes his family "liars and cheaters" because they're afraid of him. A dominating, egotistical boss can do the same thing to his workers. Both the "strong, silent" and "dominating, battle-axe" types are suffering from an inferiority complex. They feel just the opposite of strong and in control. They try to bluff their way to power. Naturally, the next rule is:

Rule Number Six: "You must strive to enrich the lives of other people." The reason the strong, silent, nor the dominating, egotistical person can't get along with people is simple. Each in his own way, is interested only in himself.

One psychologist said, "You will make more friends in a week by being interested in other people than in a lifetime of trying to get other people interested in you."

I hope these two laws and six rules gave you food for thought as they did me. Haven't you observed firsthand, probably lived with, or worked for dominating, boastful people? Doesn't it help you to understand them better? This striving for superiority is "common to all men and the source of all human achievement." But, in the end, only individuals who meet and master the problems of life, regardless of their own worldly achievement, are those who strive to enrich all others, who touch lives all around them. "Cooperation is the great shared commonplace of the human race."

If we're going to make friends, getting along with people is a must, a real spiritual achievement.

A friend and I enjoy reading tombstones. He found one in a lonely Tennessee graveyard that said it all. A simple slab of limestone. (Like myself, my friend likes to imagine the heartbroken person who put it there.) What prompted those words to be chiseled out for any and all to read? He said he thought it was a mountain widow. The letters were so crude, he figured she chiseled them out herself. The total tribute of her life to the man she had loved. "He was always considerate." That was all it said.

My psychologist friend said, "In the presence of such 'divine completeness' I could only bare my head." I know the feeling. When I read Theodosia Burr's marker, "She died of a broken heart," I wanted to weep.

In getting and keeping our friends, most people won't believe it. But. As the song says, it's not what you do, but the way that you do it. It's HOW you feel that puts other people at ease. We can't hide it. Our true spirits show in a million indirect ways: A look of the eye, inflection of our voice, touch of the hand.

You can't put people at ease if you don't want them to be at ease. If you're envious and full of hate, all the books on etiquette won't make you a companionable person. These people you want to cultivate as friends have to feel your interest and love. That's what puts them at ease.

Remember I said in a previous chapter that 25 percent aren't going to like you regardless. Twenty-five percent think you can do no wrong. The other 50 percent are still making up their minds. So relax. Be yourself. You aren't appreciated for all you do. None of us are. In fact, there's a real possibility if you are efficient in thought but deficient in love, you probably aren't appreciated at all. Some "people" prefer you to be ordinary. It makes them seem less drab by contrast.

You just might meet up with a few people who, for some unfathomable reason, are actually jealous of you. After receiving repeated hurts in my teens from one individual, my mom helped me to see the jealousy in this so-called friend.

Isn't it puzzling sometimes, why some people refuse to be our friend? Some persons, while they don't want you to be too different, don't want you to be like themselves or an echo of others. If you stole their thunder, it would make them seem insignificant. They'll have none of that. On the other hand, if you got lost in the herd, you'd be considered a dull companion. So just be yourself.

Think about it from their standpoint. It's hard to like someone who tries to be everything, you see them everywhere, doing what you would have done—*if.*

You are going to run into jealousy. You're going to run into gossip. How do you handle it? There is no sword so powerful, if you're afraid of it, than gossip. Yet none so impotent if you know it is a sham.

We all have our own ideas, opinions, and beliefs. You have to sift through a whole lot of people to find quality friends—people who allow you to have your own ideas, opinions, and beliefs, and allow you to express them, even though they might not agree.

As long as the lashes of our critics mean more to us than noise, we'll never master this problem. Every experience we have is a test of what we believe.

If we follow what we believe, and do the best we can from the basis of our standard of truth, nobody has a right to blame us. There's no other honesty, no other way to be happy.

If you live in a neighborhood that talks and talks, or work in an office that participates in this popular indoor sport, remove yourself from the scene mentally if not physically. If folks see that it doesn't bother you, that what they say about you desn't make you suffer, it will stop. No one gossips when it produces no results.

If you want to free yourself from this curse of gossip, you've got to decide what you think about gossipmongers. If you see them as vultures of a dying age who feed on the dead flesh of a body of a harshly critical person, you could smile just like you would at any buzzard on an old, dead tree.

You've seen the type. You see them adjusting painfully to the minor social requirements. They never achieve a primary purpose. They have their priorities all mixed up. Take church, for instance. The gossipers, super critical, judgmentals are there, as they are outside the church. How can you tell? Stop and listen. This is their creed: the right clothes must be worn to church. Belief in the religion taught here is not important. A bridal veil of the proper length is vital at all costs. The question of whether you really love the man you're marrying is incidental.

They're phonies. They decide on mimic values—anything to be considered "in." These super-criticals, judgers of others, have crafty consciences. You might come to the conclusion I have—reformers are the ones who need help. That's why they've taken to making the world over. History shows us when evils press within a man, it's easier to deal with faults in others.

Little souls wish us to be unhappy. It really aggravates them to see us joyous, efficient, and free. They like to feel that "fate" is disciplining us. Not God. It gives their egos wings if ours are clipped. Don't listen. They could ruin our lives in an hour if we listened to their childish, silly, immature opinions.

> I am more deadly than the screaming shell from the howitzer. I ruin without killing; I tear down homes, break hearts and wreck lives. I travel on the wings of the wind. No innocence is strong enough to intimidate me; no purity pure enough to daunt me. I have no regard for truth, no respect for justice, no mercy for the defenseless . . . My victims are as numerous as the sands of the sea, and often as innocent. I never forget and seldom forgive. My name is—*gossip!*

Chief and I had a firsthand experience with gossip. It started in church.

A dear friend called me one morning, "Libbylove, is everything okay with you and Chief?"

"Sure. Why do you ask?"

"I was at a circle meeting at church this morning and someone told me you and Chief had separated. I told them we were together at a dinner party Saturday night. (This was Monday.) I said you all looked fine to me. That Chief was telling about taking you shopping. Say, did something happen yesterday, Sunday, I don't know about?"

I laughed, "No. We went to church together. Everything's fine. Don't worry. He's weathering his male menopause just great. He's getting so much like his old sweet self, I think I'll keep him."

"Well, I thought so. But I didn't begin to worry until I got three more phone calls after the church meeting. I figured I better check."

"Thanks for caring."

I dismissed it from my mind. My friend belonged to a church across town. I had to deal with it when I started getting calls myself. One of them really disturbed me. So much so, I got in the car and went to see her eyeball to eyeball.

"Libbylove, I've heard the rumor all over town. Don't get upset because it started in my church. Your church members are talking about it, too."

That did it. I work like a trojan at my church because I love it—love my knee-buddies. But for someone there to talk about me behind my back, that I didn't like at all. So the next time we had one of our luncheons, I cornered a buddy who would level with me.

"Yeah, I heard it in the kitchen. But you know, Libbylove, you can't stop rumors."

"I can try."

The next opportunity I had was a small church board meeting. Our minister was there. After the regular business was taken care of, they asked if there was any more business.

"Yes. I'd like to know if it's true you all have been talking about Chief and me? Believe any of those stupid rumors? I heard from another church friend that my own church knee-buddies' tongues were wagging. That hurts me."

My minister spoke up. "I heard the rumor, too, Libbylove. I dismissed it. After all, you two were at church together. Everything looked fine to me. So I didn't pay any attention to it. Not worth bothering about. Don't you pay any attention to it."

My minister, my friend, and my knee-buddies made me feel a lot better. That if any "discussion" went on, it was caring. They knew better.

Chief's reaction? He laughed. He got me laughing, too. He thought it was hilarious anyone would consider a father of nine to have time, money, or inclination to indulge in one of America's favorite pasttimes—infidelity.

Well, I could laugh. But I didn't think it was hilarious. I wouldn't blame either of the two parties. However, it appealed to Chief's sense of humor, so I promised to "have fun" with some of our friends.

We were to eat dinner at our club on Saturday night. Chief set up this scenario. We were to be late. We were. He went in the front door. I went in the side door. We approached the table where our friends were sitting at the same time.

"Hi, Libbylove, how are you?"

"Fine. And you?"

Our friends didn't know whether to look at us or not. They had seen us come in separate doors. They didn't say one word, not even a greeting.

"Oh, I'm just fine. And how about the children? All doing okay? You need any money?"

Well, our friends couldn't stand it any longer. When they looked up with those startled looks, Chief and I couldn't contain ourselves any longer. We broke out in howls. They did manage to laugh a little.

"Sit down, you nuts."

"You told us to come eat with you. That you all thought we *should* be seen in public together. We're here."

After more headshaking and shared laughs, we all marveled how news travels in a week, with no competition from radio and television, just by mouth. Ever notice how often a narrow mind and a wide mouth go together? Luckily we try to live so we wouldn't be ashamed to sell the family parrot to the town gossip.

It worried our friends more than it did us. They were regular sleuths on a big case. They narrowed it down to the rumor, "a doctor in town, with a big family, lived in our section of town, was running around." Now that could fit most any town. Ours is loaded with doctors. How "big" is a big family? Our "section of town" covers a wide area.

So crisis in our marriages can come upon us suddenly. It not only takes our faith in ourselves, in our mate, and in our Maker to weather the storm. But it certainly makes for smoother sailing to have your good friends aboard.

Reams have been written since the beginning of time about friendship. After our little bout with "gossip," Chief and I enjoyed this Mark Twain quote, "It takes your enemy and your friend, working together, to hurt you to the heart; the one to slander you and the other to get the news to you."

It is said you grow up the day you can laugh at yourself. Chief and I did a lot of growing up after that little brush with gossip. Conscience is said to be a walkie-talkie set by which God speaks to us. Although our conscience was clear, we figured God was trying to tell us something as a couple. We thanked Him that we had lived the kind of public life, as well as private, that no one we cared about believed we were separated.

When someone asked Chief, he laughed. I said, "What do I say, Honey?"

"Tell 'em, sure we're separated—every day from nine to five."

I'm sure the separating and divorces are rampant in your town, too. I read somewhere that the divorce rate's making America "the land of the free." But the marriage rate's increasing, too, so that shows America's still the "home of the brave."

Friends stuck by us in bum times, so I was ready for some fun times. I dreamed up a Sexy Sixty Celebration for Chief's big sixtieth birthday. He had weathered the midlife crazies. He was mellowing, getting to be his old, sweet, bubbly self again. That was cause for celebration. All the nine were in on the surprise party.

Keeping something from Chief is hard to do. The ranks had to stick together, to not let anything seem different. We all worked together. I zapped my savings from the bank. We went to work. Each had their job:

Name tags and place cards: Toby (youngest daughter) made them. The name tags were round, black ink on white paper. The outside of the circle was printed "I am a V.I.P. to the Griffins." The inside of the circle was the guest's name. This was attached to a red ribbon.

Table decorations were done by my Emily (oldest daughter) and her husband, Kenny. Red-and-white checked clothes with all the kerosene lamps and such I could round up. A collection of old graters with a candle inside provided the lighting.

Arrangements: Randy's job. All the RSVP's were sent to his house. With his wife Patty's help, they made a huge banner to honor the birthday "boy." They mailed out the invitations: "Once upon a time, sixty years ago this December, on a Friday the Thirteenth, luckily for us, William Kimball Griffin was born at Bynum on the Haw. (When I chaperoned Toby's Girl Scout troop to England, we told Chief about visiting Shakespeare's birthplace, Stratford on the Avon. He laughed and said, "No big deal, I was born in Bynum on the Haw." Bynum is a teensy town on the Haw River.)

"To celebrate this momentous occasion, the many recipients of the one 'from whom all blessings flow' (A nickname for Chief that always gets a reaction, as we all know who the real One is—our Heavenly Father) are planning a surprise roast and toast. Chief will no doubt supply the boast."

We requested the RSVP to be sent to Randy's. The end of the invitation read, "In order for this to be a complete surprise, we beg you to keep your lip zipped and this letter out of sight until then. No presents, please. Your presence is his present."

The guest list read like "This is Your Life." Everyone we could think of that had made a difference in his life. His favorite teachers. All his friends. We were limited as we hired a hall and it wouldn't hold them all. (Chief always ends his blessings with the Irish touch, "May our hearts and our homes always be too small for our friends.")

The democratic family meetings were still functioning then. The nine had their input, too. They could invite their friends who had frequented

Bedlam through the years. School and college friends. Chief's school and college friends. Our World-War II pals were invited. The kids moved out to stay with their friends so our bedrooms could accommodate our out-of-town friends. Our guests had to "hide" at the neighbors until party time.

Chief was watching a ballgame on television when our oldest two sons walked in. They asked him to go look at some property for sale they were interested in. Chief was in sport clothes and loafers. He went with them.

At the appointed time, they brought Chief into the place under the ruse of having to use the bathroom. The property they supposedly were looking at was behind the American Legion hut. When Chief walked in, the orchestra, on cue, struck up the old tune, "Dinah." Dinah was Chief's nickname in high school. (He weighed 135 and was a blocking back. He used to say he was 135 pounds of *dynamite.*)

I was lucky to get the orchestra from 5 to 7:30. They had an engagement in a nearby town. I picked out all the songs that had sentimental attachment to our long courtship and marriage.

All the females of our family, including daughters-in-law wore long blue checked aprons over white blouses. All the males wore blue checked shirts. I bought red hearts and cross-stitched the girls' names on them. I cross-stitched the boys' names on their shirt pockets in red thread. That way, all the mob could tell which ones were which.

We had a great time with our relatives, our friends, and our children. Chief who is most verbal had to be quiet as each one, starting with our family, through that long procession of people, had a roast and a toast. Ted and his wife, Susan, had charge of the music. Randy's wife, Patty, took pictures. Ned and Debbie brought in the cake—a white job with gold crowns on it. The bevy of grandchildren helped wheel it in. Everyone was asked to bring whatever they wanted to "toast" with. Kim's wife, Mary, provided snacks. Kim, Junior, was Master of Ceremonies. His job was to keep Chief from saying anything. Chief used the crying towel frequently during the evening. Parks taped the affair. Steve had charge of "Props and Artifacts." He made posters that held clippings of Chief's past achievements.

Although I wondered how we'd ever get Chief into the place, I still had reservations as to how he would react. So I asked one of his dental buddies.

"Suppose he doesn't like it?" I said. "Would you like something like that? After all, I've zapped my savings. I'm worried."

"Libbylove, is it paid for?"

"Whadda' you mean?"

"Is the party paid for?"

"Oh, yes. I've taken care of all that."

"Well," my friend laughed, "He'll like it. I know I would if it was paid for!"

Chief did like it. He even took the cartoon I drew of him in his stride. The place cards were about the size of a dinner napkin. The event was printed on top, then the guest's name. Underneath was the agenda. On the bottom was a picture I drew of Chief wearing all the things the nine couldn't stand—a big bow tie, a wild printed sport coat, and His red-white-and-blue house slippers they threated to pitch out. I had him astride a horse. Chief wore wraparound sunglasses. (He borrowed a pair of mine once on a cruise when he couldn't find his. Didn't faze him. But the kids never let him forget it.) One hand was giving the World-War-II victory sign. The other, holding onto the horse, was holding a big fat stogie which the nine hate.

The other side of the place card was printed our version of the Moravian Blessing: "Come, Heavenly Father, our guest to be. And bless these gifts bestowed by Thee. Bless our loved ones everywhere. And keep them in Thy loving care. Amen."

After all their moving out of their own beds so we could have a pajama party, they couldn't get over the fact we and all our guests hit the sack right after the birthday celebration. "Our get up and go had got up and went." But as the rhyme goes: "We could still wear a great big grin when we thought about where our get up and go had got up and been!"

And our friends were with us all the way, through bad times and good times in the mirth and misery of marriage.

16

Dismantling Bedlam: Libbylove Vows Never to Look Back, Just Forward

"Honey, I bought a condo while you were gone," Chief greeted me with this little bit of information. I had just returned from a speaking engagement.

"Oh? Was this an investment or what?"

"Yeah, guess you could call it that."

"Come on, Chief, quit playing games."

"I thought this place would suit both of us." Chief watched me flop into the nearest chair.

"Tell me more." Was this blarney or baloney?

"It needs lots of work. But. I told Debbie . . ." I'm still just staring. "You know Debbie, the realtor, who works in number-one son's real estate office?"

My mind was in a whirl. We have Debbie, our daughter-in-law. We have Debbie who's Chief's right hand at his office. This Debbie was showing Chief a condo.

"Condo? For us?" Chief nodded.

That I had feared was upon me. It was time to leave Bedlam.

"Listen, Libbylove, I put money down. Made them an offer. It does need a little work. But I knew with your decorating ability, you can make it look good. Just think, instead of four-thousand square feet on three floors, we'll just have eighteen-hundred square feet on *one* floor."

I just nodded.

"Less to heat."

I kept nodding.

"Less to clean up."

Now he had my attention.

We had discussed moving out of Bedlam for years. Six bedrooms for two people? Ridiculous, but fun. I had a different "project" going in each bedroom. I always claimed I wanted to build. Had the lot with the type cottage for two in mind. I love to build. I like to see something come up out of the ground. Exciting.

"Mom, if you all build and daddy dies first, would you live there alone?" This question was posed at one of our family meetings.

"Sure. My mom lived by herself until she was ninety-nine. I'm not afraid, if that's what you mean."

"Chief, what about you? Would you live in the little house if Mom died first?"

"No way. I've got to have people."

"That does it, folks. A condo's the only thing." The nine agreed.

"Wait a minute. Not just any condo. I want something all on one floor. But. The main thing is location. Gotta' have my trees. Want to be on a knoll, not in a ditch. Don't want to open my front door right smack into my neighbor's. Now if you can find me that. You know, a good place to walk and swim. Good neighbors. . . ."

"Okay. We'll keep our eyes out."

Whew, I thought I had them off my back. They'd never find something that met *all* my specifications.

They did. So what was my problem? I had a thirty-year accumulation to go through. I agree with Maisie, my college roommate, that we should be like nomads. Just pick up our tents and move.

My across-the-street friend, Evelyn, had already moved near the condo Chief had said yes to in my absence. It took her two years to unload her stuff. She's a neatnik. Organized. I'm talking about a woman who doesn't know where her marriage license is, her college diploma. Me. But. Can tell you exactly where her grandmother's Bible is. How do rats unpack? What to do about it? Write about it. Here is my public confession—one of my columns, "Saving Trash and Treasures."

I am a packrat. I admit it. When our dream house was built, it had a full attic and basement to accommodate my habit.

Fellow collectors understand. Trash or treasure? Tacky or classic? Who's to judge? Who's to say? That's the question.

The answer? Tolerance.

My kids are tolerant. They look on me as the square in the family circle. I save things. Most of us do. I could usually tell which of my children inherited my packrat tendencies. One preschooler worked diligently to remove the door stops in our new home. It kept him quiet. Not underfoot. Happy.

Doorstops can be replaced. Happy children can't be. I did wonder what he did with his collection. Did he throw it away? Sell it to his brothers? Do some trading?

The mystery was solved when I found a shoebox of doorstops under his bed. I realized then that I had a 100-percent, natural-born packrat.

Through the years, he spent many happy hours scooping up leftover programs. Think of the many recitals, ballgames, and graduations that contributed to his collection.

I was tolerant. This self-confessed packrat certainly understood. Trash or Treasure? A matter of opinion.

I come from a long line of packrats. I remember the thrill of seeing a copy of my great-great-great-grandfather's handwritten will. I learned he freed his slaves. This is my American-Revolution-grandfather.

I enjoyed looking at the yellowed copy of graduation exercises at our state university. In the 1800s. About the graduation speech my grandfather's brother delivered.

The most fun of all is reading old letters. Especially my father's and mother's love letters. Learning about their lifestyles. Their thoughts. Their value systems. What a heritage. All preserved for my knowledge and enjoyment by packrats. Preserved by somebody who cared. Cared about those coming after them. Their descendants. Hopefully. Prayerfully. Fellow packrats.

They say history has to keep repeating itself because nobody listens. Not true. Packrats do. Every time I took my nine to visit museums, I reminded them how those fascinating articles got there. Packrats. Packrats willing to share their treasures with others.

My theme song? 'No packrats. No museums.'

It's true. If everybody threw everything away, if no one saved things, there would be no record. No proof. No insight. No understanding of how our ancestors lived, loved, fought, and died for us to enjoy the fruits of their labor.

What do you collect? Rocks? Stamps? Do you catch the grief I get from my nine for being a packrat? I admit it told me something when a local television station called me years ago. (Even they had heard about my attic.) They asked if I had a porkpie hat and big bow tie. When I answered yes, that I could produce these items pronto, they were amazed.

Attics can be fun. I had saved one item of clothing from each decade. The oldest? My grandmother's handmade black taffeta skirt with the beaded blouse, worn during the era of the bustle. I enjoyed wearing it to a Governor's Inaugural Ball. (With my build, I didn't have to find a bustle.)

I found everything from a flapper-style dress from the 20s right on through simple above-the-knee shifts—styles going full circle.

You noticed I used the past tense? All was going well. Now I am moving out of my dream house. Giving up my collections. Parting with picture hats. Flower-covered pillboxes. Feathered creations. Parting with old shoes. (Keep them seven years, they do come back. They are already broken in.)

I am really trying to be practical, not nostalgic. Really. After all, I took a very practical view of raising nine kids. I put a sign in each of their rooms: CHECKOUT TIME IS 18 YEARS. It's right under the sign Chief made and put over their desks. The lettering is crude. But the message is clear: THINK!

It is checkout time for me. After all, I have enjoyed being a packrat for thirty years.

Can you even imagine what it does to a bonafide packrat to watch six big dumpsters being loaded and carried away? That doesn't count a couple of truck loads that went somewhere. Don't know if it was to the city dump or to one of the kids. I was dazed by then.

"Mrs. Griffin," I looked up at the man driving the dumpster. He smiled shyly but sweetly.

"I'm a packrat."

"You are?" I felt better already.

"Yeah. . . . I read your column," he grinned. "I know how you feel."

"Thanks." I truly appreciated empathy at this point. "What do *you* collect?"

"Metal."

"Metal, like in coins. What kind of metal?"

"Any kind."

"How about all those fans under the carport?"

"Great. I'll have to come after work with my truck."

Fine. I had a friend—a fellow packrat. He and his wife enjoyed taking the leftovers. I think the three kerosene lamps I had for outdoor parties thrilled him most of all. It made me forget Saturday.

The nine waited for us to fit the furniture into the condo. Whatever didn't fit was up for grabs. They came over to help two Saturdays.

"Mom, you can't come in." Number-four son greeted me as I walked across the lawn.

I had just driven up. The place looked like we were having one of our parties. Cars surrounded Bedlam. Then I remembered it was no party.

"Mom, you can't come in." Number-four son was joined by number-five son.

They were serious. If it had been any of my other sons, I'd think they were just trying to get a reaction out of me. Not these two.

"Whatta' ya' mean, 'I can't come in?' It's *my* house."

"No, Mom. Sorry. The others said keep you out. *You won't throw anything away!*"

So I turned and slowly walked back to the car. I thought about my rest-home-bound brother's stuff that was stored in the basement. I thought about the stuff the kids had left.

Stop and Think.

We had already made the big move. The furniture was placed in the condo. The decorating job looked great. It didn't take but one day for the "big" move. I had six weeks to pack books and "stuff." The "stuff" was fourteen boxes in the den of my writing "don't you dare throw away's."

Stop and Think Again.

Just like you've never seen a Brinks truck following a hearse, you've never seen a moving van following one either.

Stop and Think Again and Again.

It wasn't the "stuff." I hated leaving Bedlam. The tears welled up as I walked to my car. It was getting difficult to see. When I'm upset I like to walk. But I knew I might meet someone. The children wouldn't like for me to. At this point I didn't know where Chief was. I didn't know where I was.

"Libbylove," the sweetest little voice called to me.

I looked up. It was a down-the-street neighbor, who's as sweet as her voice.

"My mama just had to move." She had stopped her car. I was getting into mine. "I'll tell you like I told mama. Libbylove . . ."

I was trying to keep myself together. Not dissolve into tears. Her eyes met mine—so kind, so sympathetic,

"Libbylove, just remember. *You're taking the important things with you.*"

Those words were like balm, healing oil. If she had been out of the car hugging me, it could not have soothed me any more.

I nodded, trying to manage a smile as she eased on down the street. As I drove home, I sent up prayers of gratitude for my friend, for my family, for Chief. At least we were making this move *together.* It was *not* the end of the world. It was the end of an era.

Everything has come full circle. There *is* life after children. There *is* life after a big move.

Chief was at the condo unpacking boxes. They looked like Stone Mountain. You unpack and unpack and they're still there. He looked up, smiled, said, "Come on in, Libbylove. Welcome home!"

Home is where the heart is. I looked at Chief. After many moons and bountiful babies, I knew why I married him. He still has that infectious grin. He is such fun to be with at times, and such a pain in the neck at times. I'm still so much more miserable without him than with him after nearly five decades. Like the nine children we're blessed with say, "Aren't we glad we've got him."

Of all the adventures of life, nothing tops marriage. Thanks be to God. Mine is more mirth than misery. Especially when you say *yes* to life and *amen* to love.